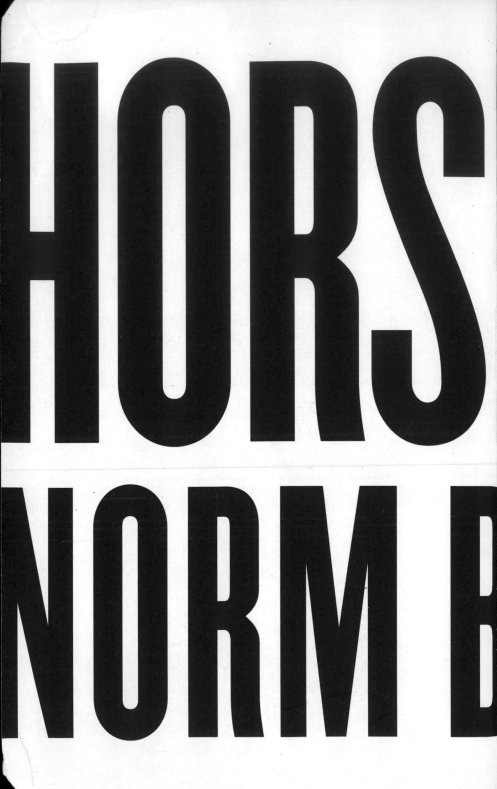

PLAY

My Time Undercover on the Granville Strip

OUCHER

Library and Archives Canada Cataloguing in Publication

BTitle: Horseplay : my time undercover on the Granville Strip / Norm Boucher.
Names: Boucher, Norm, 1957- author.
Identifiers: Canadiana (print) 20200185721 | Canadiana (ebook) 2020018573X | ISBN 9781988732985
   (softcover) | ISBN 9781988732992 (EPUB) | ISBN 9781774390009 (Kindle)
Subjects: LCSH: Boucher, Norm, 1957- | LCSH: Police—British Columbia—Vancouver—Biography. | LCSH: Royal Canadian Mounted Police—Officials and employees—British Columbia—Vancouver—Biography. | LCSH: Undercover operations—British Columbia—Vancouver—Biography. | LCSH: Heroin industry British Columbia—Vancouver—Biography. | LCGFT: Autobiographies.
Classification: LCC HV7911.B68 A3 2020 | DDC 363.2092—dc23

Board Editor: Merrill Distad
Cover and interior design: David A Gee
Cover images: "Unpaved Parking Lot, 1981" by Greg Girard
Author photo: Della Vaslet-Thomson

NeWest Press acknowledges the Canada Council for the Arts, the Alberta Foundation for the Arts, and the Edmonton Arts Council for support of our publishing program. This project is funded in part by the Government of Canada.

NeWest Press wishes to acknowledge that the land on which we operate is Treaty 6 territory and a traditional meeting ground and home for many Indigenous Peoples, including Cree, Saulteaux, Niitsitapi (Blackfoot), Métis, and Nakota Sioux.

NeWest Press,
#201, 8540-109 Street
Edmonton, Alberta T6G 1E6
www.newestpress.com

No bison were harmed in the making of this book.
Printed and bound in Canada
3 4 5 21 22 23

To Sally

CONTENTS

FOREWORD

Peter M. German, Q.C., Ph.D. Deputy Commissioner (ret'd.),
Royal Canadian Mounted Police

Life and death on the streets of Vancouver parallel what occurs in every large city within North America as a result of the scourge of hard drugs, be they heroin, cocaine, methamphetamine, other opioids, or any combination or permutation thereof. Norm Boucher devoted his policing career to working as a drug cop. He witnessed the ongoing drug crisis from a vantage point that few, other than the victims themselves and a cadre of dedicated social workers, ever see up close and personal.

Norm Boucher was a Mountie, a member of Canada's federal police force, the fabled Royal Canadian Mounted Police. But his task was not to ride horses while wearing a scarlet tunic, to drive sled dogs across the frozen tundra, or to drive code three to 911 calls. His chosen occupation within the Force and the reason he joined, was to "work drugs," as both an undercover operator and a member of the drug section.

The RCMP first began policing the drug dens and drug houses of downtown Vancouver one hundred years ago, when it was renamed from the Royal North West Mounted Police and became Canada's national police force, responsible for federal statute enforcement, including the opium legislation of the day. In Vancouver, the drug section grew over time to become a large division, composed of multiple units that pursued heroin, cocaine, and marijuana investigations, and engaged in cross-border operations. Specialized units sprouted up to better investigate these crimes. Among those was an undercover unit, composed of select members, each given a unique number, and allowed to undertake oftentimes dangerous assignments.

As an undercover operator, Boucher was highly trained to integrate within a milieu, in which addicts and traffickers live much of their adult lives. Criminality is like wallpaper in this world. It is everywhere. There is no road map for undercover officers. Developing a fine-tuned sense of survival, Boucher worked a particularly difficult beat in downtown Vancouver, a city once believed to house more heroin addicts per square mile than any other in North America. With supplies entering the country by land and ship, his job was to combat the deadly trade using his intellect, his senses, and a keen awareness of his surroundings.

Horseplay describes a moment in time in the history of Vancouver. The redevelopment of a wide swath of old tenements, hotels, and factories in preparation for Expo 86 had not begun. Vancouver had yet to be discovered by the world. In similar fashion, society was closer in time to the past than to the future. The downtown Granville Street Strip had fallen from its earlier neon heights to becoming a sleazy den of stripper bars, adult film stores, and bars. The early 1980s were heady times in downtown Vancouver and even more so in the drug scene. Hard and soft drugs were flowing through corridors of the city. Hardened police units worked the Strip in plainclothes, throttling suspected users and traffickers carrying packets of heroin in their mouths. The legalization of drugs was the furthest thing from the minds of most persons. Furthermore, as Boucher notes, going after the money generated by drug sales was an approach still in its infancy. Parliament did not outlaw money laundering until years after he worked the Granville Strip. In Boucher's time, it was all about the drugs and getting it and the traffickers off the streets.

Horseplay represents eight months in the life of a microcosm of society who spend their lives in or near a strip of seedy, rundown bars waiting for their next fix of heroin. Most had experienced run-ins with the law and were hypervigilant to the presence of cops from the drug squad as well as undercover operators. The author was already an experienced operator before taking on this assignment, which finds him starting from scratch to ingratiate himself with the addict milieu. He has no other police officers or agents to assist him, and his cover team remains at a discreet distance.

Careful not to divulge the tactics of a police officer turned hype, Boucher does provide insights into the life of an undercover officer. His role was particularly complicated during the eight months of *Horseplay* because he was dropping in and out of two worlds. Unlike deep cover officers who live away from family for a prolonged period, Boucher lived with his wife in the suburbs of Vancouver, at least on those days or weekends when he could escape the job. He also dropped in on his cover team of officers at their safe house and completed his notes and expense forms, before returning to his adopted life.

Observing that all undercover operators transition from feeling like an outsider in their undercover role, to accepting it as their new reality, Boucher acknowledges that the highs and lows of the heroin scene became his new persona and one in which he felt comfortable. He likens it to a bar. Everyone is either an outsider or a local. He made that transition at the Blackstone Hotel bar and in the drug trade operating in and around its environs. The author describes the ravages of hard drugs on a civilian population, heavily addicted and desperate for the next fix. As a police officer, his role was to arrest the traffickers and hope thereby to reduce or stem the illicit trade. It would be easy to throw one's hands in the air and ask why. It almost seems like a never-ending task, and in some ways it is. That is the life of a police officer. As one senior sergeant told me when I began my career, your first day will mimic your last. In many ways it is a thankless job in a world composed of humans, with all the frailties that we know so well.

Boucher was not immune to what was occurring around him. In fact, from the time that he first enters the Blackstone Hotel bar, it is obvious that he sees real people and not police targets. He develops a rapport with street people, hookers, addicts, those with mental health issues, and traffickers. He must duck and cover like a boxer and sometimes even take the first jab. Not only does he see real people, but he sees humans stuck in a rut fuelled by drugs. Despite this, it was his job to develop criminal cases against them and get them off the streets for at least a short while and hopefully have them undergo treatment programs.

Looking back on his career, in particular, the eight months of *Horseplay*, Boucher does not provide glib solutions to seemingly intractable problems. Instead he carefully analyzes the various approaches to the "drug problem," and recognizes that enforcement is just one aspect of a much larger societal response required to stem the daily deaths.

The RCMP has remained Canada's national police force for one hundred years, precisely because of members like Norm Boucher, who were prepared to make great personal sacrifices, risking their health and home life, in the hopes of making a difference. Working on a drug unit is not easy. It has its highs and lows and you deal with persons in every walk of life, but mostly with those who are addicted or who feed off addicts. It is dirty work. It often appears that you will never make a difference. All of these facts and sentiments are magnified in an undercover role. Very few police officers ever make this commitment and of those who do, only a few can continue in the work for long without "burning out" in one fashion or another.

Vancouver and its drug scene have changed dramatically through the years. Today, it is estimated that over 1,000 addicts die on Vancouver's streets every year due to overdoses, with no end in sight, a shocking indictment of a society in which the average standard of living is among the highest in the world.

The urgency of the problem is not lost on anyone who travels down Hastings Street as it meets Main. The response to the ongoing drug crisis, an epidemic in some communities, has largely moved away from enforcement and reducing supply to finding medical alternatives to drug addiction—harm reduction. Boucher acknowledges that this approach has its place, although it is not lost on him that reducing harm implies that harm continues. The RCMP no longer has a drug squad in Vancouver, choosing instead to direct its resources to high-end organized crime, which may or may not include drug trafficking, and to anti-terrorism priorities.

Horseplay is an honest book by a police officer turned author who seeks not to tell his story, but the story of a community and a country's response to the illegal traffic in drugs during the early 1980s. Despite the gap in time between then and now, there is one constant. Hard drugs continue to kill and continue to do untold damage to individuals and families. The conversations recorded in *Horseplay* are taking place tonight in seedy hotels and bars throughout Vancouver and every other large North American city. Seldom however have these firsthand accounts found their way into print. Quite simply, addicts and traffickers do not write books. Here however we have a firsthand account told by a person who moved seamlessly from one world into another and, with the aid of contemporaneous notes, gives us a play-by-play of life on the Strip. His account does not represent vainglory, but that of nitty-gritty life in the underworld, a world that few care much about and fewer yet will visit. Boucher has done himself and the RCMP proud.

PREFACE

Heroin. They used to call it "Horse," and it has been a part of Vancouver's history ever since someone learned to produce it for the street market. In 1983, the Granville Strip was where you went if you were looking for it. The eight months I spent with the heroin users of the Blackstone Hotel, living their life, changed the way I looked at drugs, and I knew as soon as the undercover operation was over that I needed to tell their story someday. Once past the violence, the hustle for a bigger deal, the "rips," and the search for a bigger "connection," addiction revealed itself to me in its many forms, each as different as the person it was attached to.

While I knew that this slice of Vancouver's history with heroin was important, it was never more important than it is today. To understand today's drug crisis, it may be useful to look back to where we were then, before needle exchange programs, supervised injection sites, and before AIDS decimated the drug user population. The heroin users of the Blackstone were not the down-and-out heroin addicts we see in the back alleys of Vancouver's Eastside.

They were capable and resourceful individuals, some good, and some bad, caught in a world of violence and prejudice, who lived with, and often accepted, their addiction. Living with them opened my eyes to the world of the opiate addict before the back alleys and the overdoses, a world that still exists today, but is closed to the public. The path to addiction is a lonely one, and my time on the Granville Strip gave me a window into that path.

Today's opioid drug crisis obliges us to take action in one form or another, but, to see clearly, we need to step back from the back alleys and overdoses. Addiction is a mental health condition that affects everyone in one form or another, and this is where we need to begin. I spent many years in the RCMP working on national and international drug issues, dealing principally with supply and harm reduction. But when someone asks me what I think of the current drug crisis, wondering how, despite all efforts to make it better, we find ourselves back where we began, I am compelled to look back to my time undercover, hustling the streets with the heroin users of the Granville Strip.

In writing this story, I have tried to remain faithful to the language of the period. Some of the terms used, including references to ethnicity, may exceed the boundaries of what is now deemed acceptable, but they reflect the location and the time of the narrative.

The story was recreated with the help of notes made at the time. Many of the events were also etched in my mind, being tied to feelings of fear, anger, sadness, and wonderment. I also changed the names of the people I dealt with to preserve their reputation, good or bad. Since many of the events took place in a bar, I also met a multitude of characters over this eight-month period. Minor characters, some of whom came across my path on a daily basis, were recreated to best convey the collective impact they had on me, and to provide a faithful reconstruction of my experiences on the street. My role undercover was to observe and capture criminal events as they occurred, but my aim with this story is to bring readers along the human side of this journey, with the expectation that they will come out of it with their own experiences.

Finally, I am proud of my thirty-five years of service as a member of the RCMP. I value the work we did during my career, and have great respect for the organization. While my story aims to portray accurately the events and atmosphere of the time, it in no way compromises any techniques of investigation.

Ottawa, Ontario
December, 2019

VANCOUVER, JANUARY 1983

I pull the heavy door open and see them for the first time, sitting with their backs against the wall, exactly where I was told they would be. They throw a short glance at me as I walk past them to a table near the bar. I order two drafts. I am nervous as hell, but I have worked for weeks to prepare for this, poking needles into the veins of my arms, and building a story to go with it. And it finally has meaning.

It will take time before I get anywhere close to them, so I take a sip of the cold beer, and try to decide who is dirty. Rick Crowley is sitting alone and, like the other hypes, no longer pays attention to me. I can't really tell if he or the others are dealing, but it really doesn't matter because I'm not going to score heroin tonight. I'm here for the long run, and I only want to be seen, get a feel for the place, and give them an idea of who I am before I become a threat to them. It also feels good just to see their faces.

In his late twenties, Crowley is the youngest. His ice-blue eyes are wide open and dart toward any movement, like the eyes of a cat.

I know that he is violent and sneaky. I also know that Captain Kangaroo, sitting alone at the next table, has over forty years of criminal record under his belt; that Kitty Baker, chatting with a group of as yet nameless hypes, is streetwise and has been around for a while; and that Cindy, her small frame hopping from table to table, is violent. There are a few stories of knifings for fifty bucks and of undercover officers being beaten up. Everybody's record says they know the game: robbery, drug trafficking, theft, fraud, and violence all centred on heroin trafficking. To a cop, it's a world to dive into where the line between good and bad is as clear as the surface of a dead pool of water. No ambiguity. They hate you for what you represent and you hate them for what they are. The Granville Strip is full of people who would rob and kill for fifty bucks, and finding myself in this greasy hole, inside the big pulsating city, makes me feel good and scared.

I watch everything they do, how they sit, and how they talk to each other. It isn't enough to understand them. I want to be like them because this is going to be my home for the next couple of months. It has been two years since my last operation, two years of shirt and tie work in an office full of cops, and I know that it will take me a while to feel like I belong.

The heroin users stare nonchalantly at the scene in front of them. They don't pay attention to each other except for a few words here and there. Each has a glass of beer on the table. The beer has lost its foam, but it allows them to stick around for a while.

For my first day in the Blackstone we picked Welfare Wednesday, the day people get their welfare cheques, and the place is filling quickly. Bartenders in white shirts work behind large jars of pickled sausages and eggs, to pour draft beer from frosty taps into trays of empty glasses. The music is getting loud and the crowd louder, as waiters begin to hustle briskly from tables to bar and then back to tables. Ninety-five cents a draft, and when a buck is given, they keep the nickel.

NORM BOUCHER

An ashtray sits on Crowley's table and he taps his cigarette against it. I walk by his table to go to the pay phone and he looks at me square. I'm the intruder and this is his place, but I know who he is, and he doesn't know me. That counts for something.

Picking up the receiver, I take a deep breath and begin to relax. I look around me and let it all soak in.

People come in through the front doors and from the alley through the back door, some of them after smoking a joint. All over the bar, small round tables are covered in red terry cloth to soak up the spilled beer, the same terry cloth I have seen in every bar of every small town I have been in, working undercover from Kamloops to Fort St. John. Months of work going from small town to small town, from lumber towns nested in thick forests amid the dark Pacific mountains, to the dusty towns of the cold plains of the northern interior, with their pumpjacks looking like strange, dark birds stubbornly stabbing the ground. There is toughness about the people in these bars. Not the kind of superficial and rehearsed toughness you see in fist fights, but a higher level of self-sufficiency. You have a feeling that they do not rely on their town to keep them going, but that they are what keeps the town alive. Vancouver is different. Like most big cities, people come to it because they want a piece of it.

At the far end, near the small dancing area, you must climb a few steps to get to the pool tables. A few people sit, sipping their beer while waiting for their turn to play. As in most bars, the patrons surrounding the pool tables keep their attention on the game as they await their turn, their quarters lining up on one of the edges of the tables. Playing pool is always a good way to get into a bar crowd. I like the game and, being a little shy, I often use it to get into the local scene. Nothing like sinking the eight ball, taking a sip of beer, and then waiting for the next in line to come and play. And when you lose, you sit and talk, and it goes on from there. I am tempted to go over and lay a quarter on the table, but it would take me too far away from the heroin dealers, so I decide to go at it cold somewhere else.

In the middle of the floor, thick cigarette smoke rises above a number of tables pulled together to accommodate a large group. Partiers who appear to know each other well, couples coming down to the Blackstone to blow off some steam, hear the music, and have some beers. They don't interact with anyone else so I'll probably not see them again. I figure it best to stay away from the centre of the room. I need regulars, people who will remember me, and with whom I can connect tomorrow or the next day. Regulars usually have a favourite table in a corner of the bar. They don't hang out somewhere in the middle. I look at the older couple sitting at a table next to mine. I didn't think much about them when I came in and they don't seem to have anything to do with the heroin dealers, but they are having a good time, and they seem to know a few of the regulars.

Looks to me like a good place to start.

WELFARE WEDNESDAY

I turn around on my chair and ask the woman if the Blackstone brings bands in.

"Sometimes on the weekends, but not like they used to," she tells me in a gentle, amicable tone.

The man at her side leans over. "They had a great band a couple weeks ago, but you have to come on a Saturday."

We talk about music for a while. I like them. They are easy to talk to and I am enjoying their conversation. Their names are Sky and George and they are from the Sunshine Coast, a short drive and a ferry ride north of Vancouver. Sky has long grey hair framing a sweet, friendly face without a trace of makeup. George is in his fifties and wears a ball cap with the letters "CAT" on the front. Both like to chat and pretty soon I lay out pieces of my story for them. It's a simple story, where I mix elements of both my real and fake life, adding to it as we talk, but not too much; this is a happy welfare day celebration, and no one cares about where I come from or what I do. They order another round and buy me a beer.

I move my chair to their table and look around me. The place is packed and the music loud. Like most of the other patrons who come down to drink and party, Sky and George aren't in the bar for heroin, but the time I spend with them gives me a chance to get a feel for the action of the place.

Everything is quiet on dealer's row. Captain Kangaroo's short white hair, combed down flat over a broad forehead, and his thick, silver moustache have earned him his nickname. Like the children's TV character, he has a good face, but it contrasts with the mug shots I saw of him back at the Shack. The first one, black and white, was taken in the sixties, and it shows a cocky young man with a full crop of dark, short hair, thick and ruffled at the top. He stares at the camera with a smirk on his face, like a roughed-up version of James Dean after a night binge and a bar fight. The other is in colour, taken a few years later. Older and thicker on the jowl, his eyes are droopy and expressionless. I know that there are many more photos of him in the Vancouver police files.

More photos are pinned to the wall. On these mug shots of heroin dealers, you can see smiles in some and anger in others; there are bruised eyes and cut faces, but mostly the despondent look of people going through a process they want to get over with. I have looked at them every day for the past three weeks. I don't know for which crime these pictures were taken, robbery, drug trafficking, or assault, but they are all heroin users and I know that many of these pictures were taken on a day when they would have gone cold turkey on a hard jail cot.

Two hookers come and sit with Crowley. They exchange a few words with him, their eyes darting everywhere in the bar. Crowley shrugs. One of the hookers, a tall and skinny woman with long dark hair and a severely pale face, looks away in the distance with her mouth open as if pondering something of great consequence. She then rummages through her purse and does her makeup. Soon after, a middle-aged man with curly hair, dark framed eyeglasses and wearing a dark long overcoat and a scarf—looks like a big firm accountant—comes in through the front door and sits comfortably at their side without saying much. They wait.

With one foot pulled back on the seat of his chair and his hand resting on his bent knee holding a cigarette, Rick Crowley watches the comings and goings. He is relaxed and his wiry frame and rounded back give him the catlike, athletic quality of a street fighter who has never spent a day in the gym. He watches the doors, the crowd, people walking in and people walking out. He watches their shoes, their jewellery, and their eyes, and whenever they walk in, who is the first person they talk to in the bar. Only after he's seen that does he let go of them. They all watch: the Accountant, the street fighter, the old man, and the hookers. They are clean now, but they know that they will be dirty soon, and that the cops will be watching, faceless among the crowd, or through the eyes and ears of informants working off a criminal charge.

I wave at the bartender, drawing a circle over the table with my finger. A short while later, the waiter, a small skinny man everyone calls "Red" because of his red hair, which he keeps greased back Elvis style, drops a round of beer glasses on the table. He pulls the change out of his apron and I tell him to keep it.

Against the wall, the heroin dealers look as comfortable together as a working crew taking a break on the side of the road, and I begin to wonder if I will see any action during the night. When two Street Crew members come walking in, the dealers look away nonchalantly. As in any other bar, these cops and the ones in uniform are the only things getting in the way of drug users in the Blackstone. Their main job is to jump street drug traffickers and turn them into informants. They know the dealers well and are feared by them because they are good at getting to a dealer's throat before he or she can swallow the small bundle of twenty-five heroin caps they keep in their mouth while dealing. I know that if they ever jump me, I'll have to open my mouth wide before they force it open with a set of handcuffs. Heroin takedowns are violent because everyone plays the game, the users on one side and the cops on the other. Not like grass or coke, where anyone, doctor, lawyer, or salesman, can pull out a hit at a party, or where a dealer in a trendy bar will approach the cops with a cocky smile and offer them a drink. There's no pretending with heroin, no hypocrisy. No one trusts you in this hardcore drug scene unless they first see you fix. It's straight crime and violence and I like the idea of being here for the next few weeks. These user-dealers have the cops in their faces every day; they must turn down people they don't know on a regular basis, because the cops keep sending in new guys pretending to be junkies on what they call "buys of opportunity." Any mistake and they're back in Oakalla for a few months. And mistakes they make. The heat is everywhere, cops and informants doing deals in back alleys and surveillance teams watching the doors of the Blackstone. They have to watch for it even when they are not carrying anything, because getting jumped by the cops is hard, and they need to treat newcomers wanting to buy heroin as if they are cops or informants just to make it through another day without going to jail. They don't party like the rest, the junkies of the Blackstone.

The cops walk slowly by Harry Bell's table and say something. Harry says something back and they walk away with a smile. Captain Kangaroo takes a drag off his cigarette and watches them walk away.

Back at my table, loosened up by beer and friendly talk, George, Sky, and I talk about grass. Drug talk is a good way to size each other up in a bar. You can tell if someone is a player just by the language used and how much he or she knows. Casual drug talk also lets you gauge the level of trust that exists between you and the others and how far you can go. First you talk about getting high, then you get on about the good Mexican Red Hair you tried a week ago. After that you talk about prices and weight and whether you have a good supplier.

So we talk about these things and soon George wants to know if I want to get in on a quarter pound of marijuana with him. I decline, but to me the work is done. Getting known as a drug user is where I want to be on this first night, even if it's not heroin. I've already spent three hours, drinking, laughing, and talking, and for a guy who a few weeks back wore a shirt and tie and worked on the seventh floor of the RCMP headquarters, that's as good as it's going to get.

Rick is now sitting by himself and the Accountant moves to a seat next to him. They both look ahead, a couple of words are spoken and the Accountant gives a nod to the two hookers. The hookers walk out behind him on their way to share a needle somewhere dark and quiet.

The heroin has trickled in like water seeping into the bottom of a freshly dug mud hole. I can't tell how it arrived, but it's good to see the action and learn from it. There is always something to learn when you sit and watch people working. I see how close everyone is together, each looking out for the heat. How they come in, sit, and make a deal with one or two words. Some hardcore users are easy to identify with their skinny bodies, colourless skin, and tired faces. Others are overweight and some even look healthy. If I met them on the street, I would never guess that they are junkies. They're all different, but they play under the same rules and everything works. Heroin is the one thing they have in common and it is what brings them here. They don't even need to speak to each other. They come in, sit, look around, and leave.

"Here's Chico!" George announces suddenly with a hint of excitement he tries to smother. A short man with wild hair and a scruffy beard walks over and leans in, resting his hands on our table. He glances at me, but speaks to George.

"The guy wants twelve and there's nothing I can do. I don't make any money," Chico says.

"It's got to be skunk ...like you said," George replies.

"Not just skunk. It's the best skunk around!"

After some discussion, George agrees on the price and everyone is cheery and talking about weed.

"You from Montréal?" Chico asks, having picked up on my French accent.

"The West End," I say.

"You probably like hash. I know where to get some.... Hash is hard to find in Vancouver, but the leaf is real good."

Despite his name, Chico doesn't have any Spanish in him, but he is short and has the dark eyes, beard, and hair so the name fits him. I learn that he is from back east and likes to talk about the scene and his connections in Montréal. I try to imagine Chico in his teens, with his thick, wild hair, wearing a black leather jacket with silver zippers, working the bars on the Saint-Denis Strip, dealing hash and mescaline, and hanging out with the other drug users on Saint-Louis Square.

"I was thirteen and I used to go to that guy's place, up that staircase in the alley," he says with a grin. "He had dropped out of school, was my supplier, and he had no furniture. He was always lying down in a sleeping bag on the floor, and every time I came by a good-looking girl was in it. Every fucking time! I remember that sleeping bag on the floor. That's where I wanted to be, right in there with the girl."

I laugh. I tell Chico about this kid taking me to a house where we met a mescaline dealer who was also sleeping on the floor. The bedroom doors had been replaced by rows of beads hanging down. We had cut school and there he was, maybe seventeen years old, sleeping on the floor at two in the afternoon. We laugh about that. Like a lot of the stories I use when I work undercover, this one is true. I learned on that day that my friend was putting out mescaline at the school. He eventually cleaned up and I have since learned that he became an air traffic controller.

Chico looks at a pair of uniforms who just came in and who are now talking with the bartender.

"The cops never came in the bars in Montréal. Not like here," he says. "Once in a while they did a 'descente' and took over the bar, but they had better bring lots of cops. Then everyone threw their stuff on the ground so it didn't matter. But they never came in alone. Not like here. We owned the bars in Montréal."

"I remember one time," I say, looking at George, "there must have been a pound of hash on the floor, and at least fifty hits of acid."

Chico and I talk about the bars in Montréal. I was just nineteen when I left Montréal to join the RCMP, but before leaving I had worked as a student delivering beer to the bars across the city, so I knew them well.

Chico looks at the two cops strolling around the bar.

"Look at them. You never see that in Montréal."

But this is Vancouver and there isn't a bar in town where one or two cops cannot get in and shake things up. Only a few blocks away, BCPLACE sits on a construction site like a freshly laid egg, while the grounds of False Creek are being torn up to prepare for Expo 86, still three years away. The city is getting ready and they tell me that this undercover operation has something to do with it, that they want to clean up the image of the city. They call it an intelligence probe, just to see how many hard drugs are being peddled on the street so they can get a handle on it. Calling this a probe takes the pressure off, but to our team it's still about buying heroin and turning informants.

Vancouver is an open city and its neighbourhoods aren't carved up by local gangs. Even when someone settles a drug account with a murder, the backstory is kept within the drug squad offices, where the names of known drug traffickers keep coming back through informants. Everything is low-key, just like the sixty-foot sailboats and decommissioned trawlers that bring in tons of weed from Thailand. Old heroin importers, many from the Eastern Bloc, have settled in Vancouver with connections in Hong Kong and Amsterdam, and spend their nights in illegal gambling joints. There is also Chinatown and its murky rackets from which emerges once in a while a middle-aged dude holding a paper bag filled with heroin. All of these people are informally linked to organized crime abroad and at home, but not much comes out through the media. The bikers are more organized and show a more public face, but they aren't blowing each other up over territory. There isn't a speed culture in Vancouver, at least not like back east, where it has triggered violent gang wars in Toronto and Montréal, their narrative splashed all over the newspapers. Everything is up for grabs. No one has control and the Vancouver cops keep a good handle on things.

Sky barely listens to Chico. She is not interested in hash or the Montréal scene.

"Good marijuana and mushrooms, all organic and locally grown, that's all you need," she says with a smile. "I love the mushrooms. They grow everywhere in the valley. Have you tried them?"

She pulls out a plastic baggie with about a quarter ounce of the tiny long stemmed mushrooms and shows it to me. "I picked them myself," she says.

Chico has ordered another full tray of beers. "Let's go outside," he says to George after dropping a few bucks on Red's tray.

The two of them stand up and George asks if I am coming. I follow them and, on our way to the back door, I'm glad to see Chico walk over to Captain Kangaroo's table and say a few words to him. Once back with us, Chico nods toward a dark corner of the alley.

"We gotta go a bit further because the cops like to come out through the back door," he says.

We walk down the alley past a few clusters of people and team up with two more guys who are known to George.

Chico lights up a joint.

"This stuff's pretty good," he says. "It's from the same supplier, but the stuff I am getting for you is even better."

"It's always better!" says George. "Ever heard of 'the stuff coming is shittier'?"

George lets out a big laugh and everyone goes along, including Chico. Chico's eyes open wide as he takes a big puff off the joint and holds the smoke while looking at me sideways, his eyes watering.

"You interested?" he asks, after letting out a trail of smoke.

"Maybe another time," I say, taking the joint.

The two guys are from Surrey. They ask Chico about the weed.

"Skunk, all buds, real sticky, I'll give you a good price...."

They exchange telephone numbers.

Everyone in a bar has a job even if they don't work. I learn that the two guys work in construction and have been laid off. They ask what I do.

"I'm a roofer, tar and gravel," I say.

After I had been laid off from the brewery in Montréal, I took up roofing as a summer job, and as soon as I knew that the RCMP had accepted me, I quit school and kept on roofing until I was hired, which was about a year. The work was hard and dirty, either scraping off old, degraded, and heavy tar and gravel, or laying clean paper on 500-degree melted tar. From early spring you took your shirt off and accumulated small burn scars from drops of tar hitting your skin. In winter, you had the wind coming at you full blast, especially atop the high-rises. But I liked the hard work and I liked looking over the city from the open roofs. It also made my RCMP training easier.

There was a raw culture among roofers that made them different from other trades. The first time I came close to someone who had done jail time was on that job. The guy was a hard working, twenty-two-year-old from Kedgwick, New Brunswick, a logging town. He was a talker, full of stories of stealing vehicles, being chased by the cops, and he told these stories with great delight, as if they were centrepieces in his life and everything else—jail, roofing, and his hometown—were just background. When he decided to return to New Brunswick, I sold him my car, an old Datsun, for thirty-five dollars. The starter was gone and you had to push the car to start it. He liked the car and I never saw him again.

My days roofing give texture to my stories and a way to build my character without getting into drug talk. After chatting a while about construction work, I tell Chico that I would see him later about the marijuana, thinking of how much work it had taken me two years before, in places like Mackenzie and Dawson Creek, not to get my face busted for a quarter ounce baggie of weed.

We walk back and Chico goes ahead of us.

"Where did you get the runners?" one of the Surrey guys asks, looking at his bright white running shoes.

"They're top of the line. I can sell you a pair for twenty bucks."

"No thanks, I don't fucking jog."

Chico doesn't jog either, but he is a drug runner, so he runs ahead of us. He's dynamic, knows the prices, and handles thousands of dollars' worth of drugs for everyone else, taking all the risk and never making much for himself.

"Look at those fucking running shoes," George says looking at Chico run ahead.

I look down the dark alley and see the silhouette of the short, wild man with big bushy hair skipping in his brand new, white Nike running shoes. I don't know what the others see in it, but we laugh all the same.

On the way back in, I use the washrooms where a good puddle has formed around the urinals. A drunk comes in and takes a free spot next to mine. Staring at the wall above the urinal, he asks if I've got into trouble yet. I say "Not yet," and he says "Too bad," but that there is still time and to hang in there. We both laugh. Back at our table, George is jovial and asks again if I want in on the marijuana. I say no, but ask if he has connections for "horse." I know that Chico heard me, but he remains quiet. George takes a pause shaking his head lightly. Heroin isn't his scene.

"Just ask around," he says. "I don't touch it."

Chico doesn't react. For the first time tonight he is thinking that I could be a cop.

"You don't look like a junkie," George says.

"I just chip once in a while."

"Don't know anything about it," he says again. "Grass is my scene."

Chico's head is steady, his eyes looking ahead of him without focusing on anything. He is listening and I know that he could help me if he wanted.

George tells me how, after Sky had given birth in their home in Merritt, he buried the placenta under a marijuana plant. "It gave it psychedelic properties," he says, his bloodshot eyes wide open. Chico is looking at me. His eyes scan my clothes. I'm glad George is changing the topic.

"I don't know if this weed's got placenta in it, but it's fucking good, man," I say.

I can still feel Chico's eyes on me as I chat with George. We are good on pot, but heroin is a whole new game, and I don't want to become the new guy in the Blackstone asking about heroin. If Chico gets up and walks over to the dealer's table, I might as well pack it in. These few tables are my only reason for being there, and I don't need the setback. Maybe I should have let the night sink in and get to heroin in its own time. Whatever happens next, Chico is the first one to see who I am and he has the key. It had to happen, and I'll just need to manage it.

"George and I are saving money to move to the Gulf Islands," Sky chimes in, "where everything is green."

"Yep, perfect for growing your own," George says laughing. "Everything is so green cops can't tell the difference from their heli-copters." A few more people come in and sit at our table and we drop the drug talk. It is close to midnight, the music's good, everyone has a good time, and George, Chico, and I go out to smoke some more. Looking relaxed and happy is all I'm looking for. When we return, George and Sky decide to hit the dance floor to David Bowie's "China Girl" along with a few smiling drunks and other couples who have found the bright spot in the night, when the day is over and forgotten, and tomorrow hasn't begun. It's a good feeling, for a moment, listening to Bowie's plaintive voice and watching the action. Later on, as I leave the Blackstone, a fight has started, and the waiters begin to kick the drunks out. Some of the couples, who earlier were dancing and laughing, are now yelling at each other. I walk by Rick Crowley and Captain Kangaroo on my way out and neither is looking around anymore. Both on the nod, bathing in a comfortable blindness, their contracted pupils and heavy lids are barely letting the light in.

Outside, the cold air clears my senses as I walk down Davie, across Seymour, and then across Richard where teenage prostitute boys stand on street corners. I pass the empty warehouses of Yaletown and continue to an abandoned rail yard, near the black waters of False Creek. This is to become the site of Expo 86, but for now, it is just a gravel strip of land surrounded by warehouses called "the Flats." The cover team is waiting for me. There isn't much to tell, but it's good enough for a first night. Chico isn't known to the cover team and they will do some checks to see if he has a record.

It's still early and we have time to go to the Skids, where the homeless, drunks, drug addicts, and small time crooks hang around when they don't have a connection. The Skids are only a few blocks away, but they are viewed as an embarrassment to a city where a world exposition will soon be held. It's the only reason why they need to send me there, to show that they are doing something about it. Because there isn't much heroin on the Skids, this is going to be a side job for us and I am prepared to buy pills and anything else a down-and-out heroin addict might buy.

The team leader looks at his watch. It's late winter in Vancouver and the cool wind makes us turn away, so he cuts the talk short and we make our way to the Skids.

A HARD GAME FOR A HARD DRUG

I get into my car and drive off. I am alone again and it feels good to be on a job. There is no better feeling than the beginning of a new undercover operation, to put on a new skin and live as someone else. Even with all the rules, and the notes, and preparation for court, there is the freedom. Freedom to create someone new and to deal with whatever is thrown at you in the best way you can. A new operation is like a book you buy and carry home with all the anticipation of a new beginning, with its new characters, each with their own story.

Six months before, this is what the two drug guys standing before me had to offer. The corporal was a tall, imposing man with a bald head and a thick Fu Manchu moustache. He had with him a young guy who seemed athletic and strong, and they leaned back in their street clothes against a desk in my office, while I sat in my suit and tie and listened to what they had to say.

"A street job buying heroin on Granville Street ...a two month job working with hypes," said the corporal, referring to heroin addicts.

"Any problem using a hypodermic needle?" his partner asked.

"I don't have any problem with needles," I said.

"It'll be a hard, dirty job, and you'll be on your own ...you're going cold, without an informant, something we haven't tried before with the hypes in that part of town ...you'll spend a lot of time in the Blackstone."

The Blackstone. I was already familiar with the notorious Blackstone. When you drive across the Granville Street Bridge, on your way downtown, this solid, six-storey hotel sits on the right just past the corner of Davie Street. Like the Yale, the Austin, and a number of other great hotels built at the beginning of the twentieth century on what was once called the Street of Lights, the Blackstone now rises above a mix of one and two-storey buildings housing adult book stores, cheap apartments, cafés, and stout bank buildings built of grey stone, their pillars having stood the best and worst of the young city's history. Well past their prime, these rundown hotels offer rooms on a monthly basis to hookers, street drug traffickers, junkies, and rounders looking for action. Most people drive by the big, vertical neon sign without noticing it, but the Blackstone is known by virtually every heroin addict and drug investigator across the country as the heart of the Vancouver heroin scene.

What I liked the most about this undercover job was how straightforward it was going to be. Infiltrating the street heroin scene on the Granville Strip meant fighting crime head on. I wanted in on the machinery that brings the drugs to the street. I wanted to get behind the curtain, look at a heroin dealer in the eyes, and get him to hand me the drug. The whole idea of being a cop is to stand on the line and deal with what's on the other side. And what's on the other side is a hard game for a hard drug.

I did undercover jobs before, buying weed, coke, and acid, but this one is different. Hanging out with heavy drug users every day isn't easy. Working without an informant to introduce me means I'll have to spend long hours with paranoid heroin addicts, to build my story brick by brick. It will be long and dirty. The Blackstone is known for its tough players and closed culture. It's the place to start if you want clean street heroin and not the crap you get off the back alleys and bars of East Hastings. It is brought in through a tight network of dealers, old-time junkies who know the business and operate under the kind of trust you get by sharing a cell in the penitentiary, or a needle in a rundown hotel room. Vancouver's connection with heroin runs deep and the Blackstone is at the heart of it, pumping blood into this network of users and dealers.

I joined the Royal Canadian Mounted Police six years ago. Growing up in the suburbs of Montréal, I knew the RCMP mainly for its work on drugs and not for its uniform. Undercover work is what I wanted to do from the start. I didn't use drugs in my teen years, but it was all around me in school, and on the streets, and I accepted it. Some of my friends were selling it, but I turned down the joints that came my way at school dances. Like many families, drugs and alcohol also left their mark on the people I cared about. That's why I joined. I've seen people get hurt by drugs, and a side of me wants to get in there and do something about it.

After training in Regina, I was posted in White Rock, British Columbia, a bedroom community just south of Vancouver. I realized then how much of a role drugs and alcohol play in daily police work: late night calls, fights, people who steal, and bad car wrecks. I worked there for three years in uniform before getting my first job undercover, working in countless bars up north and in the interior of British Columbia to get in with the local drug crowds buying weed, hash, acid, and coke. After this job, I took a break from undercover work and found a job in a general investigations section in Vancouver's headquarters, a tall, white office building near the airport we call the Ivory Tower. This is where I was in shirt, tie, and clean, short hair, when the two drug guys assessed whether I would fit in on the streets of the Granville Strip and Vancouver's Eastside.

It took a few weeks to let my hair grow out and study the

heroin scene. "Everyone knows the game on the Granville Strip," said Smitty, a city cop who has spent years working on the Street Crew chasing the junkies of the Strip. The Street Crew is made up of RCMP and Vancouver City cops who specialize in taking down street-peddling traffickers. By turning informants, the Crew takes more drugs off the street than large target teams working for months with telephone intercepts and surveillance. They get dirty every day of the week, hanging around dark alleys, jumping hypes, and getting search warrants. They also use their informants to help other units, like robbery and homicide. Everything on the Granville Strip is about informants.

Most heroin arrives in Vancouver in ounces and kilos, as pure as it gets from the labs of Asia and Europe, usually through Hong Kong or Amsterdam. Some of the brown heroin comes from the jungles of Colombia and Mexico, but most of it comes from Asia. The best heroin Vancouver has to offer is China white, or "number four" heroin, over ninety-five per cent pure when it starts its journey across the Pacific. "Number three" is next, with its brown tinge and seventy per cent purity in its uncut stage. An ounce of "pure" heroin in Vancouver will already be cut, from as low as thirty-five to seventy per cent, and will cost between $12,000 and $16,000. None of that matters much to the users because, by the time it reaches the Blackstone, the heroin will be cut down to anywhere between one and six per cent.

Even if they are fighting for scraps, the junkies are a tough crowd to infiltrate cold, so I knew that I would need to have a story they could understand and believe. Then I would have to bring something they want to the table. This is how it works on the street, whether you are in Vancouver, Montréal, or in the rough bars of Northern British Columbia. This is how it works in any business.

Smitty and I talked a lot about the junkies of the Blackstone, how they speak and how they fix; how they ordered their beer and how they drink it; and how they can tell if the product is good. I practiced tying up my arm and fixing, cooking milk sugar and then plunging the needle into a vein of my arm. I did enough of it to leave some tracks on my arm, helping the process by slipping blood under the skin so it would leave a bruise. Most junkies like to "mainline" heroin, by injecting it directly into their veins so they can feel the rush, but others prefer to "skin pop," which means injecting the heroin under the skin so that it can be absorbed slowly by the body.

And the language. Syringes on the street are called "outfits," "fits," or "rigs," and a capsule of heroin is called a "joint." And if they sell you bad stuff, or steal your money during a deal, they call that a "rip." If that happened, you say you got "ripped," not "ripped-off."

"You can call heroin 'smack,'" Smitty said, "or 'H,' or 'junk.' You can even call it 'horse,' like they did in the old days ...or you can just ask if 'anybody's got' and they'll know what you're looking for. This is a junk bar, they'll know."

Smitty has been a cop on the Strip for many years and he knows most of the dealers. He also knows their scams. "No one will sell to you unless they see you fix," he said, "and they will rip you off if they get a chance ...or they'll take your money on the front and disappear ...or sell you some fancy sugar like lactose or dextrose ...or they'll take you somewhere and rob you."

None of the cops on the Granville Street beat will know who I am, which means I'll have to watch for them any time I score.

"The cops and traffickers can both hurt you if you don't keep your head up," Smitty continued. "Not much we can do to help you ...it's all about instinct. Don't get into people's faces, even if you get ripped. And if you're jumped by the Street Crew, relax and open your mouth to show you're not carrying anything, or to let them retrieve the heroin if you're dirty. They won't fuck around."

Like the rest of the cover team, Smitty is level-headed and I had a good feeling about him the first day I met him. That's the way it is with cover team members. I have nothing but respect for every cover team member I've ever worked with. They are part of a special group. Not every cop is like that.

"If someone rips you, you have to hurt them ..." an RCMP member told me before the operation began, "...otherwise, they will hurt you." "Sure," I said. The man was a team leader on the Street Crew and he liked to carry a non-issued gun in an ankle holster. Hyper and nervous, I could see him lose it in a takedown. Fortunately for me, my undercover team is made of solid members who understand that undercover work doesn't depend on how you dish out violence, but on the strength of your character. I threw out his piece of advice. I don't know much about heroin, but I know about people and people are what undercover work is all about. A strong character makes people think before they act against you. A good cover story brings them on your side. What I needed to do before anything else was build myself a life story that I could own and feel, and then dress and act in a way that would fit with the story. Everything else has to follow from that.

THE SKIDS

"There isn't much heroin here ...nothing but pills and chemicals," says Smitty in the dark, empty parking lot.

What I like most about Smitty is that he is pure cover. He has no interest in going undercover. He's also a member of Vancouver's Emergency Response Team and he likes to look after the undercover operators. He knows when to give support, and when to give advice, and he knows the difference. The kind of guy who takes you aside to tell you that you are drinking too much or asks if you need a break.

"Don't follow anyone out of the bar, let them come to you. They'll kill you for your buy money," he says, referring to the thirty-five dollars I carry inside my boot.

"Just let it go if it doesn't feel right," another cover man says.

The other cover man is also a trained undercover operator, a marathon runner with a million-dollar tan who just finished a high-level cocaine job. He's high-strung, and like most operators, he understands the power of the mouth and how quickly it can get you in or out of trouble.

I turn my back on the cover team and make my way to the rundown hotels of the Skids, tucked in between Chinatown and Gastown. The wind is cold and I shiver under my waist-length leather jacket as I turn onto Hastings Street and see the colourful neon signs of the Sunrise and Brandiz. Like the Granville Street hotels, the Sunrise and the Brandiz hotels were built at the turn of the century when Granville and Hastings were the main arteries leading to downtown. City builders and businessmen came to these hotels when the city was still trying to figure out what it wanted to be, and later on, these signs lit up the comings and goings of miners, oil workers, and fishermen who came to Vancouver to blow their hard-earned money on women, booze, gambling, and a warm bed.

They are now beacons for drug traffickers and drifters. Granville and Hastings are still the main way to get in and out of town, but the hotels have faded away from people's consciousness. On Hastings Street, cars drive by the Skids on their way to a show or dinner at Trader Vic's in the downtown Harbour, and no one pays attention to the drunks, hard drug users, and street criminals walking in and out of the beer parlours.

I cross Hastings Street and try to concentrate on who I am, hunching my shoulders as I approach the bars, but my vision isn't clear. My clothes smell, my hair is messy, and I know my cover story well, but I don't really feel it. There's still a void in my head about how I'm going to fit in. I look at the people coming in and out of the bars, and fail to see a pattern or a countenance I can latch on. I am a good mimic so I just figure it will come to me once I am inside the bar.

I walk inside the Brandiz and look around me. Heads turn. I pick a table near the far wall. The place smells of sweat and stale beer and the music is loud. People come and go, relentlessly looking for something or someone. Serious conversations, some laughs, many are drunk or high. After a while, I begin to figure out the regulars who seem busy with one hustle or another. In the centre of the bar, a girl in jeans and a tight T-shirt talks to a biker type in animated fashion. Her skin is yellow and her dirty hair is pulled back into a ponytail. She speaks in bursts, in between taking long drags off her cigarette. The man waves his hand to dismiss her and she leaves in a hurry. She later comes back with two men and the four of them confer at length. When they leave I turn my attention to the other tables. The action keeps going with one deal of some sort or another, but none of it matters to me. This is the end of the line for most of the rounders in this bar; they are desperately looking for a score, and I feel my drive and ambition fading away.

I am almost halfway through my beer when someone mutters at a guy walking by.

"I'm gonna fucking kill you."

The guy ignores the threat and walks away. The threat came from a man sitting at a table near mine. He looks around, angry, and turns his stare in my direction.

"You fucking asshole," he mutters.

I look away.

"You're a fucking asshole. You hear me?"

I ignore him. The man is getting loud, but no one turns around. It's as if there is only the two of us in that corner of the bar.

"Fucking asshole," he barks again, still looking at me.

I have no feel for this, so I decide to stay put and ignore him. But on the street, everything you do counts for something and even doing nothing is doing something. I make eye contact.

"What are you looking at? You fucking prick. I'm gonna fucking kill you," he says again.

He stands and pulls a knife out of his pocket. I slowly get off my chair with my beer glass in my hand.

"You're fucking dead," he says.

I glance at the blade. No drug deal, no arrest; he's not even after my money. This mentally deranged nobody wants to kill me and there is no story to it. I wasn't prepared for that. No rip, no drug buy, just a guy with a fried brain. There is no sense to it.

He moves closer. Doesn't even look drunk. If he were drunk, I would be in a better place to deal with him. I tense up and everything else is blurry. My back is to the wall and there is nowhere to go.

He takes another step.

If there is one thing I learned working in uniform is that you have to be the one raising the ante. I throw my beer glass at his face and grab his wrist, pushing him back hard a few steps while holding his wrist as tight as I can. I go for his throat with the other hand. He seems disoriented and falls backwards over the table, me on top of him. I look down at his right hand, the wrist of which I still hold tight with all my concentration and might until I see the knife drop onto the bench. I see a woman's hand take it and put it in her purse. Now that I can turn my attention to his head, I hit him with my fist once, and again in the jaw. It's over as quickly as it started. I feel myself being pulled back. The crowd gathers in and I am surrounded. "What happened?" Asks a voice in the crowd. "He had a knife," says a girl, pointing a finger at me. I recognize her as the woman who picked up the knife from the bench.

A wiry guy with a pockmarked face and bad teeth approaches and looks at me square.

"You want to fuck with a shiv?" He brings his face close to mine. "I'll show you a fuckin' shiv," he says as a group of men begin to gather around me, looking for an excuse to pound on somebody.

I am soon surrounded by an angry mob and I know that I am finished if the beating starts. The wolf-pack mentality is settling in, ominous and threatening, its silence more dangerous than the guy with the knife, who now sits alone on a chair, dazed, and looking ahead in some faraway place. All I have to do is move against someone and it will be over. Someone might hit me first, but it's out of my hands. I am scared, but unlike facing a guy with a knife, I am paralyzed-scared because I have nothing to focus on.

"Who the fuck are you?" I hear someone ask.

"What are you doing here?" asks someone else.

You can duck a baseball, but you can't stop the rain you see coming at you so I stand there silent. The crowd feels it too, as if it is slowly realizing that it is now expected to act. I am a new face, and alone, and it gives them strength and purpose.

"You're fucking with the wrong people," someone says.

Then, I hear a calm voice speaking at my side.

"I think you better leave."

The waiter moves in between the crowd and me. I look at him, as if he had awakened me from a bad dream, and take a few steps back. Everyone is staring as I turn around and make my way out of the bar.

Outside, I walk down Hastings, a bit hunched over, my eyes darting around me. I see two men come towards me on the broad sidewalk. Their hands hang at their sides, empty. They walk past me, and as I glance back to see them walk away, I am hit by a gust of wind. I take it full, feeling its blast on my face and on my chest. It was always a tough neighbourhood, where people die for no reason, and no one cares, and I feel like I finally understand the place. I skip across Hastings amid the busy traffic and it occurs to me that the air doesn't feel so cold anymore.

GREASY SPOON

The next day in the early afternoon I return to the Brandiz to see if I can find the man with the knife and identify him to the cover team. I walk around, but do not see anyone I recognize. I am prepared for some form of challenge or threat from the regulars or the waiters, but no one either remembers anything or seems to care. As if to make a point, the morning rain has washed the grime off the sidewalks. It's a new day on the Skids.

The cover team plans to keep looking around for the guy in the next few days, but I am just as glad to move on. I now feel that I am a part of the scene and I don't want anything to get in the way. The fear is real and it gives me substance.

Our work done at the Brandiz, so we decide to move back to the Granville Strip and I welcome the move away from the Skids. The clouds are dispersing and the late winter sun warms my back as I walk to the Blackstone; this is the kind of afternoon that makes you forget months of cold rain and dark days. I smell the city and cannot wait to connect with Chico again and get back to where I left off. He has a criminal record for selling heroin and his picture is now pinned to the wall of the Shack. He seems to know a few of our targets and, even if he doesn't trust me, there's a connection between us.

I am also hoping to see George and Sky again, talk about drugs, and maybe meet other established rounders. I will likely not do business with them because I'm not interested in weed, but I still wouldn't mind the company.

I pull the heavy door open, and once inside the Blackstone, I have to adjust to its new face. Except for old Palmer, a known pedophile heroin addict in his sixties, and a few scattered people, the place is empty. The Blackstone is now the perfect bar for junkies and dealers who need to watch what goes on around them. Without the welfare crowd, the place looks as big and bright as a warehouse, cold and dirty, the air thick with the smell of yesterday's smoke. I walk around the bar under the watchful eye of Palmer, who is nursing a beer in the corner against the bar, his black cowboy hat pulled down on his brow. Being by myself isn't good so I pretend to be looking for someone before making my way out and across the street to Jerry's Café.

Inside the small café, where heroin addicts congregate late in the night, a series of vinyl covered booths line up against the wall, in the style of a 1950s diner. There's a food counter at the far end of the narrow restaurant with a menu plastered on the wall. Nothing in the café suggests that I am going to have a good meal; the place is dark, the walls drab, and the atmosphere nonexistent. It's a real hype hangout where deals take place at all hours of the night, but I am alone and it is still early in the afternoon. A man and a woman behind the counter stare at me. I recognize Kitty Baker, a local heroin dealer in her late thirties. I look up at the menu.

"I'll have the stew," I say.

Kitty looks at her coworker who presents a blank face. He opens the lid of a pot sitting on the stove and pokes around inside with a wooden spoon as if to stir up some living creature. He looks back at Kitty and shakes his head.

"You don't want the stew," she says in a tone that totally convinced me.

"What about the fried chicken?" I ask.

"It's not ready," Kitty says, looking at me as if I am being unreasonable.

I leave the café feeling like a schmuck. As a lost tourist on a budget, I would feel fine, even thankful that they did not feed me their salmonella-infused stew and would have just moved on, never to return. But as a heroin addict who tries to look like he belongs— like he's got street smarts and can move and shake—not even being able to score food is pretty sad. I walk across Davie to the Austin, with my hands in my pockets, and see the crowd gathered around the stripper. I take a seat at the front and order a beer. It doesn't fit my role to be there—hypes don't care much about strippers, nor spending too much on a beer—but I want to be somewhere where nobody will pay attention to me while I figure out what to do next. On the stage, the dancer spreads her legs for a man who has pulled out a flashlight.

I finish my beer and leave the Austin. Outside, the city hums under a darkening sky as the rush hour begins. Most cars leave the downtown core, crossing the Granville Street Bridge; others head to the West End and the Lions Gate, determined faces alone at the wheel, each with a place and family to go to. Soon, the downtown core will be empty and the drug users will return to the Blackstone.

I cross Davie Street, passing by a group of office employees waiting at the bus stop, and enter Theodore's in the St. Helen's Hotel. The place is dark and quiet. Located almost directly across from the Blackstone, it is considerably smaller, but it has more character and you can go there and enjoy the place and the music any day of the week. You may be able to find heroin if you ask around, but Theodore's isn't really a heroin bar. It's a good spot to play pool and talk to the average guy out for a drink, so I walk in, chat with the waiters, and work on my story. After putting in a good measure of face time, and letting one of the waiters know that I am interested in buying some stolen stereo equipment he has a contact for, I walk across the street to the Blackstone again. A few people have settled in, giving the place early hints of the life to come. I pick a table in the centre.

I DON'T FRONT MY MONEY

The Blackstone doesn't have an atmosphere of its own. It's a box with tables covered in terry cloth and a couple of pool tables. It doesn't bother inviting strangers in. Doesn't bring strippers in. You come because you want something, to see someone, or, on a quiet afternoon, because you want to be left alone with a glass of beer in front of you. The Blackstone takes on the face and character of the people who are in it, regular old-timers, hookers, drifters and rounders, and heroin users and traffickers.

Soon, sneaky Rick Crowley, old Captain Kangaroo, and the nasty girl with the pretty face named Cindy come in and huddle at their usual table. They sit together against the wall, the row of their faces matching the row of pictures pinned to the wall of the Shack. Two uniformed cops walk up and take Crowley to the washroom to shake him down. The other dealers look on with hate on their faces. There isn't a "why?" or an argument from Crowley. If he were a coke fiend in a coke bar, he would argue for his rights, or at least put on a show. Hypes don't argue with the police.

If I had an informant working undercover with me, I would be able to get into this crowd at once and build my own network from there. But without an informant it will take time to make them believe that they need me more than I need them. If I go to them and they tell me off because they don't know me, I might not be able to get back in before the operation is cancelled. Time is my biggest challenge even with the heroin dealers sitting no more than twenty feet away from me. I know their names and what they did time for, but before anything else, I'll have to make them believe that I have something to offer.

Crowley returns and shares a laugh with Kangaroo who shakes his head. The bar returns to its heavy tranquility. I need to find my own place in the crowd.

I finish my second glass of beer and order two more. I was told that beer was ordered in twos at the Blackstone, just like the heroin caps. When your beer is almost down to the bottom, you pour it into the fresh one and switch glasses. That way, you never taste the last, tepid swig, and you never reach the bottom. The cold, full glasses arrive and give me comfort. The idea is to be seen and the way things are going I don't expect to be doing a deal any time soon. I put heroin out of my mind and get comfortable just being a bar rounder.

I place a quarter on the edge of the pool table. A couple of guys are playing and I team up with one of their friends. After a chat and some joking around, they invite me to sit at their table. I sit next to a large man who has white plaster dust in his hair and stains all over his clothes. He has a good, hard face, a smashed-in nose, and his loud laugh comes straight from the belly. He buys me a beer and I'm glad to be part of something. When Chico comes in with a man I had not seen before, I wave him over.

"How's it going?" I ask.

Chico leans on the back of the empty chair next to me. "Good," he says while checking out my company.

I tell him about the fight I had at the Brandiz.

"You shouldn't go down there," he says, pulling the chair next to me while his friend takes a seat across the table.

"Someone pulls a knife on me he'd better finish the job," the drywaller interjects before getting into a story about a fight he had and showing everyone the scar he has on his abdomen.

"That guy doesn't pull knives anymore."

We talk about how quiet things are.

"My friend here just got out of jail," Chico says, "...needs Valium."

The man holds his shaking hand above the table and tries to steady it.

"First day out ...I know what that's like," the drywaller says. "I got something for you. Let's go outside," he adds, placing a marijuana joint on the table.

We go outside to smoke the joint, and when we return, Chico leans in.

"Can you spare me some change?" he asks, looking at me with a faint smile.

"How much do you need?"

"About twenty."

"I can't. I want to score myself a cap tonight."

Chico lets the words evaporate in silence, but it feels good to know that he wants something from me. His gaze drifts around the bar.

"How about a fin, then? I'm a good player. I can beat these guys. I just need the money to get going. I'll give you your money back and then I'll buy the beer. I can beat these guys."

I give him the five dollars and Chico smiles. He walks to the table and before long he is playing and sharing a laugh with a group sitting near the pool table.

Meanwhile, I hear a crash from the other end of the bar to see Rick Crowley stand up and punch a guy fast and furious. The guy folds under the avalanche of blows and falls down to his knees. Crowley keeps on hitting him and finishes him off with a few good kicks, aiming for the head. The guy gets his arms in the way, but he appears stunned. Everyone at my table is looking at them and I feel my heartbeat go up. The drywaller smiles.

"That's what you gotta do. Hit first and then hit, hit, hit."

He grabs his buddy in a headlock and fakes a few punches to his face. When he lets go, the buddy manages a weak smile, his face red, and his hair messy.

The fight over, Red rushes in with another waiter and grabs the bleeding nose guy by the arm. They escort him out while Crowley sits down and curls one leg back under him on the seat.

"Stupid fuck!" Cindy screams in a raspy voice at the guy as he reaches the door.

"Yeah, you tell him!" the drywaller yells back. He laughs and leans into me.

"I bet she's a fucking tornado in the sack," he says, "but I wouldn't touch her with your dick. She's a junkie. What a fucking shame."

"What a body on her," I say. "She's probably just chipping. Junk isn't bad if you know what you're doing."

"You do junk?"

"Yeah, I tried it. I do a cap once in a while."

"I wouldn't fucking touch it, man."

He pulls out another marijuana joint.

"This is what chills me out."

Cindy comes over to our table to bum a cigarette from one of the guys and soon breaks into a raspy laugh.

"That's because I'm too much woman for you," she tells the guy rubbing her small frame against him.

I know that Cindy's boyfriend is doing time for robbery because his picture is pinned next to Cindy's on the wall above my desk. The letter "V," for "violence," has been written below each picture with a felt pen.

The action at the dealers' tables has picked up. Palmer sits at his regular table, closest to the bar. He has people sitting with him while others come and go. I've been told that Palmer was once caught picking up underage prostitutes and is well known by the local cops. Next to him, Crowley sits back on his chair and is now counting a roll of bills he pulled from his jacket pocket. Kangaroo has left the bar, but Cindy stays at our table, chatting with two of the guys.

At the pool table, one of the players takes aim at the eight ball and announces a bank shot.

"Hit the fucking thing!" yells the drywaller before swallowing half his draught.

The player moves the cue briskly back and forth. Veins bulge out of his tattooed arms as he leans against the table.

In a bar, there are two kinds of pool players. The first kind hits hard and thinks little; the other kind hits lightly and thinks hard before the shot. The tattooed guy belongs to the first group. The eight ball hits violently against the pocket sides, but doesn't sink in. Meanwhile, the cue ball smashes into the thicket of remaining balls before disappearing quietly into a corner pocket. The drywaller barrels out a laugh.

"You fuckin' numbskull, I knew you'd fuck it up!" he yells, laughing.

"You're up," says Chico giving me back my fin.

"I'll skip this one," I say as I tense up my shoulders and neck in a light shiver again.

Chico sizes me up with a glance, then shrugs and returns to the pool table.

I turn to the drywaller. "You think that girl can help me out?"

"What?"

"I'm looking."

"Looking for what?"

"H, Man ...horse."

The cover team warned me about Cindy, but I am pumped up by the fight and the beer makes me see things clear and simple. The drywaller turns to his buddy and the man shrugs before turning to Cindy, who is still standing with a knee on the chair. She looks at me with interest and comes over.

"You looking?" she asks.

"Yeah," I say, giving it a light shiver for effect.

"How many?"

"Just one."

"Give me the money."

"No way I'm fronting my money.... How much?"

The girl rolls her eyes. "Thirty-five ...what do you think...? Give me the money!"

"I don't want to do it that way."

"I don't even know you. I'm taking a chance because you look sick."

Cindy takes a drag of her cigarette. "Do you want it or not?"

"I want to see it first."

"I need the money if you want me to help you. I can see you're sick, man. It'll only take five minutes ...the guy's right there."

"I don't front my money."

"Listen, everybody knows me here. My name is Cindy. What's yours?"

"Nick."

"Listen, Nick, it's only five minutes away. People know me here."

"I don't front my money"

"You're wasting my time." She stands up ready to leave.

"How far do you have to go?" I stammer.

Cindy crosses her arms. "Listen, are you sick or not! I'm just going across the street then back. Five minutes."

I played sick and it's too late to back out. So I throw the book away, reach into my boot, and with the confidence of someone buying a Persian carpet at a street market, I give her the thirty-five and watch her disappear.

I fronted my money.

THE RIP

The pool players finish their beers and leave me waiting alone in front of a dozen empty beer glasses. This isn't good, but I still don't want to believe that I've been ripped. It's not the thirty-five bucks, it's the embarrassment and the heat it would bring on me. And I don't want to think of how the cover team would react. A buy or a rip can happen to anyone on an opportunity buy. Then you just leave, and all is well, and you start again the next day somewhere else. But a lot has been invested to get me here, so everything has to make sense for the long term. My credibility is more important than the buy itself and I can already feel it crumbling away.

Sitting alone in front of my warm glass of draught beer makes me look like a mark. After waiting a while, I am propped up by a faint glow of hope when Cindy walks in through the back door. I look straight at her as she walks toward me, feeling good and hopeful, but she turns before getting to my table without even looking at me and sits with a group of rounders.

I wait a few minutes and try to figure out what to do. Seeing that my options are limited, I go to her table. She pulls away from the umbrella drink she is sipping.

"It's invested," she says looking at her friend across the table.

The table turns silent, everyone looking at me to see where I am willing to take this. I go back to my table, alone again.

A short while later, I go to her again.

"I want my money back."

"I can't …it's invested."

"I want my money back," I say again.

Her friends stare at me.

"Like I told you, it's invested," Cindy says, sucking air bubbles through her straw.

"What do you mean, it's invested? When is it coming?" I hear my words scratching the air like dust in a sawmill.

"The guy got busted and I lost it."

"So you owe me."

"It's invested and it's gone. I don't owe you anything," she replies, getting back to her drink.

"She doesn't have your fucking money," one of her friends says, making good eye contact.

"So why don't you fuck off!" throws in another man.

The first guy glares at me in a way that invites me to go with him while Cindy quietly chews on the pineapple piece still attached to the umbrella of the drink she bought with my money. The only umbrella drink in the whole fucking Blackstone.

So I let go and walk away, passing by Palmer who looks at me under his black cowboy hat, narrowing his eyes, and by Crowley, who is by then on a heavy nod after having sold his lot and shooting up his share. Once again I feel small, my money's gone, and I have been pegged as a mark. I am tired and the beer has given me a headache. Outside, it has rained again and the air is thick. Granville Street is covered in a wet black coat and the street lamps make the fog glow around them, forming blurry globes suspended in the dark. I walk by the old and tired warehouses of Yaletown and make my way to the flats, the old CP rail yard filled with dirt, where the members of the cover team wait for me. The rip is only for thirty-five bucks and they don't say much, but it's embarrassing as hell and I know what they are thinking.

STEPPING BACK

I have two shirts for the job. They are both blue and made of cotton. I wear one of them every day under my blue leather jacket, the lining of which is beginning to give off the acrid smell of sweat, which the shirts pick up in between washes. My goatee has thickened to a tuff of brown, red, and black hair growing in different directions and curling back into the skin. It's itching and a few pimples have turned to scabs. To compensate for the nerves, a bad diet, and the beer, every afternoon I manage to play racquetball with some members of the cover team. Then, I shower without soap and get dressed. I like the jacket. It feels worn and comfortable and it smells like work.

The rip was a setback and to Cindy I am now a mark, an outsider, but if the cover team is feeling shaky about where this is going, they aren't letting on. Back at headquarters, usually on Monday mornings, the brass sit around a table to go over operations, decide whether to pull the plug on anything that isn't going anywhere, and assign the freed resources to something more promising. Monday has gone by and I am still here, so we are given another chance. I never liked the business side of drug operations, but this one is in my hands.

I enter the Blackstone and walk by Cindy without even looking at her. I look around and see Chico. He nods and smiles and I sit at his table.

"How's it going?" he asks.

"Good ...I got wasted last night."

Chico pushes a beer my way. I look around.

"Anything happening?"

Chico shakes his head. "Pretty quiet."

"I wasn't gonna come downtown, but I gotta find somebody who owes me money," I say.

"Where are you staying?"

"I'm out in Burnaby, my old lady's got a place there. Takes me twenty minutes to get here."

"I know people in Burnaby," Chico says, probing.

"I don't do anything there. My old lady doesn't know what I do. She fucking talks too much."

We drink the beer, then walk out to the Austin Hotel across the street, and I pretend to look for somebody. Chico follows, but he doesn't ask any questions. We keep walking together, hitting the bars to see if we'll come across anyone we know, hoping that something will come of it. Chico and I get along, and even if he doesn't know it, he is helping me get by my incident with Cindy. She doesn't know how well I am connected to Chico and that's enough for her to stay away.

Someone in the RCMP told me that I needed to be aggressive, even violent, to deal in the Blackstone if I wanted to maintain some form of respect on the street. But I am learning that being a heroin addict on the streets has nothing to do with respect. It's about hustling and getting by without getting your head kicked in. That's what Chico and I do, walk around hoping to sniff out some opportunity. He doesn't trust me, but if I turn out okay, he might make money out of it. As for me, fronting my money to someone like Cindy was a stupid move, but I need to keep going. I am new in town and am taking my lumps like any other heroin user.

As I walk along with Chico, I decide to work on the small things. The cover team has given me a beat-up yellow Datsun 510. It reminds me of my first car and fits who I am. And my clothes are dirty, but they're mine. I put aside what other policemen have told me about drug addicts and I begin to look within. What kind of hype would I be? Everything I know about heroin I have learned from others: "Hypes talk this way"; "they use drugs like this"; "hypes are violent"; "this is how they think." But this is me and I have to figure out myself what kind of hype I am to become.

I usually park in the alley behind the St. Helen's Hotel, across from the Blackstone, on Granville Street. That's my parking spot. I am not yet a heavy addict and I sometimes buy a heroin cap, just because I like it. That's my story. My car. My apartment. My life. My own addiction. And if you know me, you know that you can find me in any of three bars: the Austin Hotel, on the southwest corner of Granville and Davie; the Theodore, or Theo's, in the St. Helen's; and the Blackstone, where most of the action takes place. You may not know yet what I do, but you know that I will be there, often sitting with Chico. If things are quiet, we will sometimes walk a few blocks toward the bridge and check out the Yale, but for the most part, we walk several times a day between the three bars, at the corner of Davie and Granville, chatting among the soft drug users, like George and Sky, or some of Chico's other friends. These bars are my home. I say hi to people I meet more than once, and play pool with outsiders who come in for the beer. I want people, heroin users and others, to get used to me cruising the bars in my blue shirts and leather jacket and it's all beginning to add up.

A few days later Chico is broke and I tell him that I have nothing, so we walk up the stairs to his apartment in the Blackstone

Hotel. The small room has a dresser and a single bed. The paint is peeling off the walls, but I'm surprised to find the room organized and tidy. Chico picks-up a crumpled five dollar bill and some coins off the top of his dresser. We walk down to the beer parlour and he orders beer.

"I went to Prince George a couple weeks ago," I say. "Do you know that a cap of horse up there goes for fifty dollars?"

"Yeah, and its not even good," Chico says.

"I tried one and it was shit. I didn't feel much."

"The best is right here. You're wasting your money up there."

"You can make good coin in George. I know a lot of people up there ...solid people. I bring them a half pound of weed sometimes ...and I make good money."

"I can get you some weed, any amount you want."

"I'll let you know next time I go...."

Chico and I drink some more and play some pool.

DEEDEE

At five in the afternoon, the Blackstone is quiet and I'm sitting alone when Chico walks in with a man in a black leather jacket and turtleneck. They stand near the door, Chico's bright eyes darting everywhere from behind his scruffy hair and beard. Once his eyes have set on me, Chico gives me a quick smile, and he and his friend come directly to my table.

"This is Luke," Chico says as he and his friend sit down.

I extend a hand.

Red comes over with a full tray of beer and drops six glasses on our table. I lay a fin on his tray and Chico fishes a dollar out of his jeans pocket while Red waits, his knuckles resting on the table. I've picked a spot between the heroin dealers and the pool table, where I know people will come. It will be easy for me to chat with a few of them, and act like I am connected. Red scans the bar.

"Tonight's gonna be busy," he says. "It's gonna be a good night!"

Of all the Blackstone staff, Red is the friendliest and seems to be the only waiter willing to acknowledge the heroin users, often chatting with Rick Crowley and Harry Bell. The other waiters barely tolerate them, looking away as they wait to be paid.

Red walks away and I take a sip of beer. Around us, the place is filling and it's good for me to be seen with Chico and his friend. As he usually does, Chico wants to know if I have any action going.

"I have someone coming later on," I lie.

Luke is sitting sideways and looks away at the people in the bar to let us know that he is staying out of whatever business we are into. He has bloodshot eyes, stubble on his face, and looks like a night owl in his dark outfit.

We settle into a discussion about stolen stereo equipment. Chico says that he and Luke can get anything I want.

"How do you know Chico?" I ask Luke.

"We met in Gastown ...at the Europe Hotel. I did some things for him."

Other than being a tourist attraction, Gastown is the hangout for the Montréal hash and speed crowd. These close and connected French-speaking guys from Québec hang around there in their black leather vests, with girls in frumpy clothes and no makeup. Beads and silver from their last trip to Morocco encircle their wrists and necks.

"Do you know people here?" I ask.

"I never come here ...too many cops. I don't even touch drugs. Don't like the heat. I'm a thief."

I stare at him. A thief? No drugs?

"That's what I do," Luke says, as if he had read my mind. "I'm a thief. J'suis un voleur."

I hear the pride in his voice and see it in his eyes.

Chico becomes giddy. "If you need anything, we can get it for you. TVs, VCRs, anything you want."

"What do you mean, like, in the box?"

"No no no, not like that, but only top quality," Luke explains, his wary eyes settling on me. "I don't do stores. I take it from good houses, only the good stuff from nice houses ...Bose, Kenwood, Sony ...I can pick any lock I want in about thirty seconds, sometimes people are even in the house."

"You're crazy, man."

Luke takes a sip of his beer. "...and if I have time, I make myself a lunch in their kitchen while they're sleeping," he adds with a smile.

I laugh.

"I can be real quiet. It's all about taking your time. I never hurt anybody. I'm a professional. I'm a thief, that's what I do."

"I tell you. He's fucking crazy," Chico says with a laugh.

I imagine Luke, the ultimate loner, coming across Canada from Montréal, getting into people's houses during the night, making himself a tuna sandwich while everyone is sleeping. Then selling his stuff in the bars of Winnipeg, Regina, and Calgary.

"I have a set of lock picks if you're interested," Luke says, pulling the tools from his pocket. "Fifty bucks and its yours."

He hands to me the two thinly filed pieces of spring steel. A basic handmade set, one piece is straight with a notch at the end while the other is flat with a ninety-degree bend in it.

"I don't really know how to use them," I say, giving them back.

"It's real easy once you get the hang of it."

"Come with us, we need someone to stand six," says Chico.

I am tempted to go with them and watch for the police while they break into houses. Being part of their group would give me credibility and I can certainly use it. But it would take me away from the Blackstone so I decide to stay with my story. I don't need to work for two street hustlers.

"I got things to do," I say.

"I've got a sledgehammer and an axe in the car," Chico says to Luke. "We can go through anything with that," he continues with glee.

Luke shakes his head and looks away.

Chico turns to me. "You hit the sledgehammer right on the doorknob and pop! That's all there is to it!"

"We won't need all that stuff," Luke tells Chico. "You just need to watch the street while I work."

Chico picks up his beer glass. He is still grinning with contentment when a tall and skinny trans woman comes in and sits next to me. Her face is rough and masculine with a flattened nose and stubble. I have seen her before running deals for Crowley and the others.

"You guys want to buy Vs?" she asks in a soft, coy voice. "Fifty cents."

"They don't do anything for me," I say.

"Why do you think I'm selling them?" she says with a laugh. "How about you, Chico?"

Chico shrugs.

The trans woman looks at my two glasses of beer. "Do you have an extra beer?"

"No, but you can have this one," I say sliding a glass toward her.

"I'm Deedee," she says extending her hand.

"Nick."

Deedee rummages through her purse and wonders out loud whether someone has taken her keys. A flash of anger wrinkles her face, but she finds them and takes a sip of beer. She sits back and smiles.

Deedee and I chat and soon a frumpy girl in a short dress comes over and scores Valium from her.

"My old man is away and I need to take the edge off," the girl says to me as if I expected an explanation. She chases the Valium down with big gulps of Deedee's beer.

In the Blackstone, Valium spreads around to settle strung-out folks like the smoke a beekeeper sends down a beehive.

"Hi, I'm Wendy," she says to me, taking a seat across from Deedee.

"Remember that old guy I was with last night?" she asks Deedee.

"You mean the one with the glasses?"

"Yeah ...he's coming back tonight. Let me know if you see him."

Deedee isn't listening anymore, but rather looks toward the front door.

"Here's my brother," she says to me. "Don't tell him about the Vs or anything. He doesn't know that I do drugs."

"No problem, I don't do drugs either."

I turn away to talk to Luke while Deedee's brother, wearing a shirt and tie and rolled up sleeves, takes a seat at our table, next to Wendy.

"This is my brother Will," she announces proudly. I learn that Will works in a shoe store downtown and visits his trans sister at the Blackstone on a regular basis. Deedee is beaming at her little brother and seems proud that he has a job and doesn't touch drugs.

We play pool and chat. More beer comes and the chatter and laughter soon reach the level of familiarity, the kind that develops when people share a drink or a joint, ephemeral, but deep with intimacy. Deedee carries a purse and likes to show what's in it. There is makeup, lipstick, Valiums, and a large hunting knife. She and her brother talk about getting some girls to work for them. Deedee wants her brother to put up the money, but he is hesitant so she turns to me and asks if I want in for half the investment. She talks about getting some rooms at a hotel nearby.

"It would take about two grand to get started," she explains.

"I might be able to come up with some coins," Will says.

"I don't know anything about the business. How does it work?" I ask.

"Don't worry, I'll run the business," she says. "You'll have nothing to do but enjoy the girls."

Deedee leaves our table to run around the bar. Looking at the pool table, Will and I decide to take on the winners, so I get up and put a quarter on the edge of the table. I look around me. Every part of the Blackstone is alive in its own way. The junkies wait, the partiers laugh and talk, and the old-timers drink the cheap beer. In one corner, a few sidewalk bikers wearing black leather jackets and chains sit with their hookers at their side, and look out at the scene before them, serious and silent, as if the mere act of sitting there was their reason for being.

Waiting for my turn to shoot, a man comes to our table and talks to Chico about some stereo equipment he wants to buy. He is tall and keeps his chin up so that he has to look down on Chico. A girl stands a few feet behind. She is dark and pretty and an Afro adds character to the soft lines of her face. I shake hands with the man and he says his name is Jimmy.

"You gonna be around tomorrow?" Chico asks Jimmy.

"Yeah, I'll be around after nine. Whatever you get, I want to see it first."

"I'll come out and see you tomorrow. If we don't have it by then, it'll be the next day."

"Don't fuck me around," Jimmy says. "If you can't do it let me know."

"We got it, man. It's like ...we know where it is and everything, you know. If we don't do it tonight, we'll get it tomorrow night. You can try it and everything, you know ...make sure it works."

Jimmy and his girl walk away. A large eagle is printed on the back of his leather jacket. I see the eagle cruise the bar just about every day. Sometimes, the eagle finds a table in one corner of the bar where Jimmy will take on a "don't fuck with me" look. He doesn't hang out with the junkies, but I can tell that he is into some kind of action.

Luke and Chico manage to hang on to the pool table by easily beating Will and me. "It's not what you make, it's what you leave," Luke keeps saying walking around the table in his leather jacket, a cigarette hanging from his mouth while his tired eyes explore the green felt. They play one more team and win again, but soon give up the table, and leave the bar to find a place they can break into. Deedee is now sitting with the heroin crowd. People come and go and there is so much going on that I can't keep track of the action. The Blackstone is alive, its blood pumping into every one of its parts, its tables pulsating with activity. I see George and Sky sitting at a table covered with beer glasses. George is chatting with the two guys from Surrey. In another corner Cindy is jumping from table to table, hustling more bad deals. The action is taking control of the bar and all I have to do is keep up with it. A busy bar will do that, throw things at you, and you don't have to look or do anything for things to happen.

Red comes to our table to collect glasses, prompting Will to turn to Wendy.

"What would you like?"

"I like Champagne," she says flicking her hair.

"Champagne it is!" Will says cheerily to Red.

When Red brings the Baby Duck he makes a ceremony of it, opening the bottle with a quick jerk that sends the sugary stuff all over the table. Wendy laughs and crosses her meaty legs, prompting Will to give me a wink. They clink glasses.

"What do you do?" Wendy asks Will.

"I'm in sales," he says.

"It must be weird that your brother is now a girl."

"For me makes no difference. She's always been good to me."

"Yeah, but you guys must have done boy stuff when you were young didn't you?"

"I guess."

"That must have been weird."

Will looks at Deedee who is now coming back from the junkies' table.

"Yeah ...I guess."

Deedee glances at Wendy before sitting at our table again. Everyone around us is busy and it seems natural for me to hit her up.

"I'm looking. You know if anybody's got?" I say in her ear.

"How many do you want?"

"Just one...."

"I might be able to help you."

"Is it good?"

"The best around, but I'm taking a chance. I don't know you."

"I know, but it would really help me out," I say.

"I usually don't sell to people I don't know. Do you really need it?"

"I just chip, but right now, it would be good."

"You have to come with me and fix."

"I want to go home and fix."

"You don't look sick."

"I'm not sick, I just chip once in a while."

There's silence between us while Deedee scans the bar.

"Don't worry about it," I say. "I have someone else out in Burnaby if you don't want to do it."

I get up and walk over to George and Sky's table. We exchange a big handshake and a few laughs.

"Watch Chico," George says before I leave his table. "He can't put anything together. I never got the weed he was talking about ...had me waiting for two days."

"Yeah, okay, thanks," I say shaking his hand again before returning to my table.

I guess my meeting with George gives Deedee the confidence she needs because she leans closely into me.

"I can do it, but I need to see your tracks."

I begin to roll up my sleeves.

"Not now," she whispers looking at Will who, his arm now around a smiling Wendy, is pouring bubbly wine into their glasses.

"Who bought the champagne?" Deedee asks.

"Will did," I say.

Deedee gives Wendy a stare and a shadow passes over Wendy's face like that of a travelling cloud on a patch of grass. When Will gets up to stagger to the washroom, Deedee sits next to Wendy and unleashes a mountain of threats causing Wendy's greasy hair to fall over her face as her head tilts forward under the storm.

"My brother's not a fucking mark!" Deedee says to me as she returns to her seat.

This is the hour when people make things straight; when the chaos and the music and the beer have worked together to bring you where you are, and you now have to make a move and lay down your cards. Wendy and Will made their move, I made mine, and Deedee now made hers. Wendy whips her hair back in place with a quick nod, grabs her glass and the half full bottle of Baby Duck, and walks away to another table.

Deedee's face is still hard. "My brother isn't a fucking mark," she repeats.

"I know. He's a good guy," I say.

"Show me your tracks."

I roll up the sleeve of my left arm. Deedee moves her head closer. I worked hard with a syringe to build my tracks and I am proud of them, but Deedee has to search a bit to see them. She snickers. Seeing my tracks has lightened her mood.

"They're not very big," she says with a grin.

"I just chip." I unroll my sleeve back down.

"I have to go across the street," Deedee says.

"Okay."

"It'll cost you ...thirty-seven because I don't know you."

"Yeah, okay," I say, thinking of the two-dollar profit she is asking for.

"Give it to me now."

I decide to front my money again, but this time there is no heat, no pressure. It's as good a chance as I will get, and I trust Deedee, even if she is a junkie.

"How long is it gonna take?" I ask.

"It's just across the street."

I reach into my boot and pull out a thin roll of clammy bills, thirty-five dollars I kept ready every day for my first buy of a heroin cap. I add two dollars more for Deedee's commission, but can't understand the math. She is risking jail for two dollars.

"Do you have score paper?" she asks.

I pull a piece of tinfoil out of my shirt breast pocket and give it to her. She walks away a few steps then comes back as if on an afterthought.

"I'll pass it to you through the mouth," she says.

I look at her and shrug, glad to hear that she is thinking about coming back.

I fronted my money just like I did with Cindy, but everything else is different about this deal because I invested life into it. There is also an honest, straightforward side to Deedee that is different from the others. I take a sip of beer and wait to see if this is my last night in the Blackstone, or if this operation has a chance to move on. All of this on a thirty-five dollar buy, with a two-dollar commission.

Looking around me, I see that Wendy has hooked up with an old john with glasses, likely the one she was initially looking for. She's rubbing the inside of his thigh under the table. Further out, Red runs around with a tray full of beer while the junkies remain seated against the wall, only a few feet away, but really a long way from where I sit. Deedee doesn't go to them. Instead, she disappears out of the bar. If I am ripped off again, I know that I will never make it to that table along the wall.

Returning from the washroom, Will comes back to the table, which has been cleared by the waiter, except for my glass of beer and his half-empty champagne glass. He flops down on the chair beside me. We both stare at Wendy rubbing the old man's crotch with one hand, her free hand darting in and around his pockets like a ferret checking out the nooks and crannies of a new cage. I take a sip of my beer while Will finishes his glass of stale Baby Duck, the bottle of which sits proudly on the old man's table.

"Where's Deedee?" he asks, without looking at me.

"Running around," I say.

Will slowly stands up. "See you later," he says with a sigh.

A few minutes later, I get up to go to the washroom. I've done all I could with this job and I no longer worry about the outcome. When I walk out, Wendy is in the hallway leaning against the wall. She pulls money out of a wallet.

"How's it going?" I ask.

"Good," she says, throwing the wallet in the trash bin.

I return to my table and see Wendy's john sitting alone, drunk; he too will not see Wendy again tonight. I glance at the front door and see Deedee enter the bar and walk straight to my table. Without sitting, she plants a kiss on me. The stubble of her cheek rubs against mine as her thick tongue pushes the tinfoil wrapper into my mouth.

"It's really good. Don't do it all at once or you'll get sick," she says with a smile before walking away.

I get up and leave the bar. Once in my car, I spit the heroin into my hand. I unfold the wrapper and contemplate the tiny pink and white capsule. It was dented when the Benadryl was taken out. I feel good. I rewrap it and stuff it into my shirt pocket.

AND IT BEGINS

Working quietly behind the counter, the bartender smashes rolls of quarters against the cash register while the waiters chat on the other side. A few old-timers nurse their beer, the empty tables around them providing insulating comfort to their solitude. Except for twenty-five-year-old Rick Crowley and a few other hypes along the wall, the Blackstone is as quiet as a church between services.

I buy a pickled Polish sausage from the bartender and choose a seat a few tables away from Crowley, who is sitting alone smoking a cigarette, as calm and aware as a cat on a windowsill. When some rounder comes in, Crowley's pale blue eyes follow him as they did with me a few minutes before, his head turning steadily on a still body, watching where he goes until he is satisfied and loses interest. He takes another drag off his cigarette.

My first buy the night before has added another building block to my story, and I feel that the time is right for me to sit by myself at a table not far from the dealers. My timing is good because Deedee walks in almost as soon as I sit down, interrupting the mood of the place with her skipping and cheery manner, and after a few words exchanged with Rick, she comes directly to my table.

"Did you like it?"

"It was pretty good."

The heroin came back from the lab at six per cent compared to the two to three per cent that is regularly seen on the streets.

"I did it in two fixes like you said."

"Did you get sick?" she asks.

"Almost at first, but once I got into it, it was good."

"I knew you'd like it, but you have to be careful here if you're just starting. It's smart to try it first. I usually do three, but with his stuff, I only do two. He's pretty reliable."

"Is your brother coming today?"

"Not today. He's working. He thinks you're a pretty good guy."

"He's a good head."

"He wants to know if you want in with the girls."

I take a large bite of my pickled sausage, the taste of fat and vinegar mixing well with the beer. I shake my head.

She moans, "It's a good deal, plus you get the girls working for you!"

"I have a girl and that already is too much trouble."

"If you change your mind, he'll be here Saturday."

Chico and Luke come in and take a seat at our table. The bar is filling, and soon after, Wendy comes in on the arm of another mark and grabs a seat a few tables over. The bar isn't as busy as last night, which is good because it makes me look and feel like a regular. Back on dealer's row, Rick Crowley talks angrily to a few dealers. They are all waiting.

"How did it go?" I ask.

Luke shakes his head. "A fucking sledgehammer," he says, dejected.

"He used the fucking hammer to break the door."

Chico is grinning behind his thick beard.

"We're at the door," Luke continues, "trying to get through the garage, real quiet and good, and then he walks away and comes back with the sledge."

Chico has sparks in his eyes. "It was taking too long with those picks of yours."

"Took the door down all right, but the whole fucking house lit up."

"He he he! I didn't know there was people in the house. There was no car in the garage."

"Next thing, I turn around and see him running down the alley with a chainsaw."

Chico is laughing louder, showing teeth missing.

"His fucking running shoes have reflectors! You believe it? Fucking reflectors. Looked like a fucking Christmas tree."

"You want to buy a chainsaw?" Chico asks me with a smile.

Luke shakes his head. "Not professional."

A fight starts near the pool tables, and as most fights do, it ends as soon as it starts with one guy doing all the hitting. Red gets there with another waiter and grabs the arms of a middle-aged man who now sits in a bloody heap on the floor. The Blackstone works under the principle that if you lose a fight, you are the one who needs to be kicked out, which makes sense since it is usually easier to deal with someone who is already beaten up. The loser of this fight doesn't seem to agree, and despite being drunk and wobbly, he manages to free himself, his arms flailing like loose firehoses. Red works nervously to grab him again and, with the help of the other waiters, drags him out toward the door just as stocky Harry Bell, whom I had already met several days before, comes in with his girl.

Harry gives the man's bloody face a contemptuous look, while walking by slowly with his hands in his leather jacket pockets and a sway that means business. His girl Maggie walks a few feet behind him. She wears little makeup and the same turtleneck sweater she wore the first time I saw her, working the corner of Granville and

Helmcken. The sweater and her glasses gave her a granny look and made me question whether she really is a hooker.

They take a seat next to Chico.

"Anything happening?"

"There's nothing around," Deedee says.

Red comes to our table with a tray full of beers. To everyone around the table, this is a normal night at the bar, but to me, having Harry sit there means a lot. He isn't carrying drugs and this is why he is sitting at our tables, but his and Maggie's pictures are pinned to the wall of my office. Harry has a long record, built over years of crime in Winnipeg before coming to Vancouver, and this is a step up for me, even if we don't talk heroin.

With nervous hands, Red empties half his tray on our table and, waiting to be paid, gives a quick comb back to his greased hair with his hand. Harry gives him a twenty.

"You got blood on your shirt," I tell him.

Red looks down and gives a nervous swipe of his table rag on the blood that smears his white shirt.

"I saw that guy before at the Austin ...was mouthing off. I almost punched him out," says Harry.

"I knew the prick was looking for it," answers Red. "He wanted to take me on outside. But fuck this."

"Yeah, yeah, fuck this," agrees Harry.

"I don't need this shit."

"No. No, you don't need it."

"Fuck this."

"Yeah, yeah. Fuck this."

Red's hands are still trembling as he counts the change.

"Take two for yourself," says Harry, throwing a couple of bucks on the table.

Red winks to Harry and goes directly behind a column where he takes one of the glasses and, his hand still trembling, drinks it down without a pause, his Adam's apple bobbing at every swallow.

The fast drinking makes his eyes water. He takes the second glass.

Not far from where Red stands drinking his beer, Wendy keeps herself close to her companion, her hands feeling his pockets while her lips kiss his neck. It's a desperate last attempt to get something out of her mark, but it's too late. The man has already lost interest in her and his eyes, made bloodshot and heavy by the cheap wine, are now looking away expressionless. The crowd is getting loud, and when the lamenting tone of Boy George's "Do You Really Want to Hurt Me" echoes through the bar, a few drunks begin to dance. Wendy's mark finally breaks free from her embrace to stagger to the washroom, leaning on a few chairs as he walks by our table.

Wendy bolts to our table. "That guy in the washroom ...he's packing lots of money. He's got a stack of hundreds."

Harry surveys the washrooms for a second and turns to me. It would be easy for two guys to smack him around and take his money.

"Hurry up!" Wendy says to me glancing at the washroom.

I shake my head. Wendy moves to another table where she convinces three men to rush the washroom.

A few minutes later, the three thugs emerge from the washroom and meet Wendy at the back door before leaving with her. The mark staggers out, his eyes lacking focus. His face has taken a shade of red and he is breathing heavily, but he seems okay. He disappears into the rowdy crowd.

People walk from table to table, talk, laugh, and you can barely notice the dealers sitting quietly along the wall. I don't know if the heroin is in and I don't bother looking for it. At my table, Deedee pulls out a vibrator from her big purse and turns it on. She winks at me and touches Harry's leg with it, making him jump away.

"What the fuck!"

She lets out a big laugh and puts the vibrator back in her purse. When another dealer I know from a picture on our wall shows up and sits with us, Harry and Maggie buy six caps from him and leave.

Soon after a couple of hookers come in and buy four caps. Even Rick Crowley, who usually has a supply of his own, walks over and scores six caps without saying a word, all business.

Cindy comes by and says she wants two.

The dealer turns to me.

With this, he tells Cindy and me to meet him in the alley. I walk out with Cindy and we don't say a word. She may remember ripping me off a couple of weeks ago, but she doesn't show it.

We follow the dealer in the dark alley to a fence post. On top of the fence post, and in plain sight, sits a small green balloon tied in a knot. The guy unties the balloon and gives Cindy her two caps. He then glances left and right and gives the last one to me.

And that's how it begins.

JOINING THE BEEHIVE

I can't say exactly how it comes to be that you find yourself accepted in a group. It's not so much that you have to look and think like the rest, but rather that you act and look the way they expect you to act and look. You can be a priest in a whorehouse as long as the whores peg you as a rotten, sex-driven priest, or else, as a saviour of desperate souls. Just don't try to save their souls after a night of sex.

I am no longer a mark. If you walk into any bar of the world, you are either an outsider or a local. And if you are an outsider and have something they want, there's a good chance that you will be a mark to somebody. The dealers are beginning to accept me because they see that I have ties to some of the people around me, even if they can't tell how deep these relationships go. To make it work, I don't buy two caps as most junkies do and as I was told to do in my briefings. I buy just one. That's what I do. I'm in pretty good shape and I don't look like a heavy user. That's who I am in my mind and the story works for the junkies because heavy users like to teach new users how to fix. Heroin is the one thing they know a lot about. After a buy, I disappear to my space without a word. I don't talk much and no one asks questions; all junkies have a secret room of their own and they understand. I am no longer an outsider.

It was like that when I approached Crowley for a cap. He had been selling heroin all afternoon, doing deal after deal near my table and he was in a good mood, even friendly. Crowley is a heavy user and a nervous dealer, but I was at ease with who I am and he felt it.

"I would if I could," he said, "but I don't really know you ...maybe if I see you fix or something."

Cool, no hard feelings. Two days later, when he had a half bundle left in the back of his mouth, I went to him again, this time asking if he had seen Harry.

"You looking?" he asked.

"Yeah."

"How many?"

"Just one."

"Okay. Meet me in the washroom."

Just like that.

Crowley is violent and cagey and meeting him alone in the washroom wasn't my first choice, but I was up for it. I just had to make sure to watch his hands and look for anything that didn't fit, like a quick word to a friend before going to the bathroom, or a change of plan at the last minute. But once we stood on the urine-covered floor, near the broken sink (I never understood what kind of violence could break a ceramic sink), Crowley was relaxed and spat the bundle out right away. He looked at me in an overly affable way, the way people who have seen violence often do when it's time for friendly business.

"Have you seen the bulls anywhere today?" he asked while untying the bundle.

"No."

"It's weird, man. I haven't seen them all day," he continued while dropping the cap on my score paper.

In the following days, I kept coming back to the Blackstone and sat with my group against the wall. We chatted and waited and I scored from whomever had: Harry Bell and his hooker girlfriend Maggie; Kitty who moonlights at Jerry's Café; Sammy Price, a known dealer recently out of jail; and a few others. Everyone had his or her way, and I had to work for it because the heat is always on their mind. Some sat quietly while others were constantly on the move, but they all watched for the heat.

With Scotty, the whole thing was social. He arranged deals while playing pool and I only knew that he was a user because I had seen him once on a heavy nod. Otherwise, he didn't look like a hype. Scotty is corpulent and energetic, his green eyes framed by a permanent five o'clock shadow and a thick mass of curly black hair. He seems always happy, and when he's not on the nod, you can hear his laugh from any table in the Blackstone.

We played some pool, and after he beat me square, I walked up close to him. "Anybody got?"

"How many?" he said.

"I just want a joint."

"Just one?"

"Yes."

"I have to charge you two bucks."

"Okay, I guess ...what can you do?"

"When you live in a shoe."

Soon after, a girl sat on my lap and planted a kiss on me, pushing the cap wrapped in tinfoil deep into my mouth.

That really got to me, to risk going to jail for two bucks. But it was more than that, I guess. Sell a few and then get a free cap at the end. The two bucks also got you the beer that allowed you to sit in the Blackstone.

We meet each other daily. It feels good to be part of the group, and to look at things from the inside. A few weeks before, I was an outsider and a threat to them. Now, I am still a threat, but no longer an outsider. I am part of the pack, a pack brought together by the war on drugs. We all know why we are sitting at these tables and no one really trusts anybody, but everyone works hard to get their fix. Real hard work, every day. The hypes get up sick most mornings, fixing the leftovers from the night before, finding out who's got and watching for the heat and anything else that doesn't fit—always hoping not to get ripped off—and then fixing again.

And waiting. Always waiting. With Maggie I waited two hours while she came and went, giving me updates on where the stuff was and when it would arrive. I didn't say anything. I just waited like the others. With grass or coke, if you wait two hours for a street deal you have to be impatient and talk about the party you're going to, or your own customer waiting, and why you want to get going. No need to talk about that with heroin. We all know why we want it. You sit there sick and everyone understands. So when she was ready, Maggie and I walked out together and followed her old man, Harry, down Granville Street, keeping to about twenty feet behind him. We watched anything that moved around us until, at the corner of Granville and Helmcken, we spotted a man coming toward us and we became nervous. I was about to pretend to ask her for directions, but she turned to me and stepped in close.

"Talk to me as if you were a trick," she whispered.

"How much for a blow job?" was the best I could come up with.

Maggie didn't flinch. To my mind, asking her where I could buy bus tickets would also have been a pretty good decoy, but I thought of the many nights I saw her standing alone on that corner waiting for her next trick, and I began to understand the business side of her job. Maggie sells sex, and to her this was the most natural thing to do. It brings the cash home every day, and between that and her old man's heroin deals, they have enough to fix and pay the bills. When the man was gone, we turned around the corner and I gave her the money. Harry gave me the cap. They work well together and don't rip people off.

Charlie McKenna is an odd guy. Almost every day since the operation began, he came into the Blackstone and sat quietly in front of his beer. He has all the looks of the pothead you come across in high school: the loner with the black leather jacket, good jeans, hair longer than everyone else, regardless of the decade. To me, he is the guy who during school recess smokes a doobie alone against the back fence of the schoolyard, where no one else ever goes. In the Blackstone, this tall and balding forty-year-old man wears a mullet, and a black Fu Manchu moustache drips from the corners of his mouth. He is tall and a loner, often choosing a table in a corner where he sits by himself. People come to him because he can make things happen, but when he isn't dealing, it's almost impossible to get any type of conversation going with him. He just sits there as if he has nothing left to give. Since the first time I saw him in the Blackstone, Charlie has watched me often enough because that's all he does, watch people from his table, his bare forehead catching the light. Even when we didn't really know each other, it was okay to sit with him and not say anything. There was a kind of familiarity between us, the kind you build after long periods of silence, me watching him and him watching me, while we waited separately for our next deal.

When I first asked if he had, Charlie told me to meet him on the fifth floor of the Austin. On my way to meet him, I saw Scotty waiting for the elevator. I thought they might have arranged to rip me, but Scotty probably thought the same thing. He was talkative and nervous as we entered the elevator.

"It's my day today," he said. "The Scottish holiday ...I've got to celebrate!"

"Great!" I said lamely. Elevator talk is universal whether you're going to score drugs, or are on your way to apply for a job.

We came off to a deserted third floor and then climbed the stairs to the fourth where we waited until Charlie was done dishing out a couple of caps to a girl I knew from the Blackstone. After my deal, I took an elevator ride up to the fifth floor then back down. Once I came out of the Austin, the girl came to me and we walked to the parking lot behind Theo's where she asked if I wanted to go fix with her. I declined, but offered to give her a ride up Robson Street. We headed out all the way to Denman, where the tourists were walking lazily, and then circled back to Robson. I made a few turns I didn't need and told her I wanted to look around for heat since we were carrying.

"You connected?" I asked.

"Yeah, but my old man isn't around."

"Let me know when he is around. Maybe we can do something."

The girl kept her head looking straight ahead. "Okay, but I don't really know you ...like, maybe he'll want to do something with you, but that's his decision."

"No problem, how do you manage when he's not around?"

"I do okay. I charge thirty for a blow job, but you gotta wear a condom," she says looking at me straight and not without pride.

"That's pretty good money."

"Yeah," she said, turning her gaze to the shops passing by, "but I don't really like to work when my old man is out of town."

Whenever I deal with people in an operation I try not to get into their personal lives. With heroin it's easy because the relationship begins and ends with the drug. I don't know where Wendy, or Scotty, or Charlie came from, or how they got into heroin in the first place. I don't know anything about their family. Everyone has a story, but no one gets into it. Together, they are the last cog in a machine that brings heroin from the poppies of Thailand to the streets of Vancouver. They'll sell to anyone interested in trying it, and their fear of informants and undercover officers is the only thing standing in the way. They are heavy users, but they have to work for it because, if they don't, they'll end up on Hastings struggling for pills.

Kitty is a busy dealer, but she never works the streets and seems to have a good handle on things. She has short curly blond hair and blue eyes that carefully scrutinize the people around her. Well into her thirties, she is steady, sharp, and has the respect of the regulars. The time I went to her to score, she remembered what table I was sitting at the night before, and the table where I sat the night before that. She didn't say anything about the time I went to Jerry's Café to have some stew, but I knew that she remembered that as well. I didn't bring it up, but I said I knew her old man and we talked about him a bit.

"He's from up north, isn't he?" I said.

"Yeah, he works in Whitehorse."

She did the deal.

Don't tell a heroin addict to get a job. He or she has one and I don't know if there are many legitimate employees who work as hard every day to get what they need. Hanging out with them every day to buy heroin, I have to look out for the heat because I don't want to get my throat squeezed by the cops. And whenever I do a deal I have to make sure I'm not going to be ripped off. It makes for a full day. I also have to work to keep my stories straight and not to get burned. Like them, I watch for anything that doesn't fit, and I get tired after a day's work just doing what the average heroin addict does every day. And I don't even have to deal with the sickness.

Kitty does everything I do, but she also has to deal with the sickness. Sick or not, she has to get out there and arrange a meet to score her bundle, the twenty-five caps that she buys for around $400 and which she will sell for thirty-five dollars each. That would be over $400 in her pocket if she didn't use. That's as much as a dozen transactions for which she faces jail time just so she can get her fix. The problem is that, when you hold that much dope it's pretty easy to climb up to it and become a bigger addict. After injecting her profit into her arm, unable to cover the cost of a new bundle, she will fill the gap by selling Valium and working at

Jerry's Café, the sickness grating at her like the permanent moan of a blown speaker.

Kitty has a mix of common and street sense, the kind that help her both manage a café and deal drugs. She can comfort you with Valium when you get out of jail, or save you from food poisoning, as she did with me when I first met her at Jerry's. People come to her when there is strife and to hear her say "That's not right, you just don't do that" is enough to calm things down. You can't really bullshit her and she could be reliable if it wasn't for the habit. She was on a pretty good nod the night after she sold to me. She looked around with her eyes half closed to keep track of things, but her head dropped every once in a while and she was gone. That's her weakness. But straight, she looks at you square in the eyes and she can really take care of you if she likes you.

Women dealers often make me feel like they can see through me. This started with me in another undercover operation when an informant introduced me to his girlfriend and family. Even if she didn't say anything to me, I could feel that his girlfriend was suspicious of me. She wasn't aware of his deal with the RCMP, or that he planned to move out of town with her at the end of the operation, leaving friends and family behind. The agent later told me that she didn't trust me. She wasn't a user, nor a dealer, and I felt sorry for her. I didn't like the deal and she felt it. Like she knew something was wrong. In the end, she didn't move away with him.

Some women can size up a guy pretty quickly. I plan to be careful with Kitty. She has a good sense of what I did in the past few days and she doesn't forget. For her, it's all business. She won't forget the buy, and she will soon be talking with her old man, who will tell her that he doesn't really know me. She is likely to mention my name to Charlie and the others. If this happens, everything I've built will begin to unravel. I'm just doing what they all do, trying to make a go of the heroin life, with the lies and the scams. Except that mine don't come from addiction, and it's only going to work until the group decides it doesn't fit. Then, I will just have to watch my step. Until that happens, I am going to milk it for what it's worth. I went a long way to get where I am, sitting against the wall in the Blackstone.

PAPERWORK

It's Friday and it has been a good week. I'm well in with the dealers and can usually find a table with someone in their group. It's only nine o'clock in the evening, but I have been in the Blackstone since four and I don't see a deal coming soon, so I walk out to my car and make my way to meet the cover team.

I park in the underground and see that some of the cover cars are already parked. The cover team has rented a room where we agreed to meet and catch up on paperwork. Every week, one of the cover team members brings me my office mail, and this week I haven't had time to look at it. I am also late doing my expense reports. Today we share the facilities with another undercover team and they are getting ready to leave when I enter. They are working a cocaine file, and they start later because they need to meet their targets in the late night discos. "You're back early," says Peter, in his snappy three-piece suit over an open collar shirt.

I've come across Pete a few times at our headquarter office, but never worked with him. Undercover operators get to know each other after a while, taking part in training or talking over a beer about the different jobs each of us is doing. Peter's companion is a woman borrowed from the City police. She is young and attractive and both have athletic bodies.

"Hey," she says, "how is it going?"

"Good ...quiet night."

"Finished already? Must be nice! We're just starting."

The coke team will be closing the bars of Kitsilano and the West End, and then going somewhere to talk deals or socialize for credibility. They wear expensive clothes, gold chains, and expensive watches.

A cover woman comes in. "We gotta go. Nine-six is waiting at Richard's. He's got a target with him."

Nine-six is the other team's agent. He has infiltrated the cocaine scene and is making introductions to the undercover operators. This is saving the RCMP a lot of time infiltrating the organization as it provides instant credibility. Because of his involvement, Nine-six will also have to testify at the end of the operation.

The cocaine team leaves and I go to my empty desk in one of the bedrooms. I have some notes to make before doing my expenses. If I make a buy, I'll usually make notes for a couple of hours, drawing floor plans and writing descriptions, but today will be quick. Not much happened and I just have to make note of a few conversations about potential deals and write a few first names. I am usually terrible at remembering names in my real life, especially if I meet people at a cocktail party, but for undercover work I have it down pretty well, putting words and images together and repeating information to myself throughout the night. I usually can come back with names, birthdays, tattoos, and addresses all in one night.

I've done my notes and am still sitting alone clapping my expenses on the electric typewriter, when a cover man opens the door and drops a beer on my desk. Everyone's in and I can hear them chat in the living room. They are good, experienced members. The team leader is also an undercover operator. He has done heroin deals in Hong Kong and infiltrated motorcycle gangs. Yet, they are genuinely happy whenever I make a thirty-five dollar street deal. They are professional and understand the lonely side of the job. They won't leave until I'm done.

GOTTA WATCH THE HEAT

Working undercover means you are always pushing things to get deeper into the action. For the most part, this is what drug dealers do as well, so it usually works out. But when you push too hard, it can get back at you.

We are a couple of months into the operation and the team members are relaxed, either doing paperwork or watching TV. The building we're in has racquetball courts, so three of us go down, and work up a sweat playing cutthroat. Playing racquetball is the last thing I do before getting into my role. After the game, I shower, change into my dirty street clothes, get into my car, and make my way downtown.

It's mid-May, the sky is blue, and the air coming through the open car window gives me my first taste of the summer to come. Not the breezy air of English Bay, with its sailboats inching their way out to the Strait. This is the thick, warm air of the city, with the grit of dusty pavement and busy sidewalks. I taste it while driving on a congested Kingsway with the radio on and my elbow resting on the open windowsill. Sitting at a red light, heat rises from a city bus idling near me as I watch the pretty women cross the street. Delivery men and women in short sleeves jump in and out of trucks, and I feel good watching them go about their work. It's as if everyone has returned after spending the rainy months of winter in hibernation. When the light changes, the bus revs up its engine, and the noise reminds me of my childhood in the suburbs of Montréal. Unable to sleep in the hot and humid air, I listened to the buses going by our house, feeling good hearing the noise slowly becoming faint as they made their way down the dark, empty streets. I've always loved the sound of traffic in the city; it gives me a sense that all is well.

I take off my leather jacket, throw it on the back seat, then roll up my shirtsleeves above my wrists, uncovering my needle tracks. Once passed Main, I turn left on Seventh Avenue before taking the Cambie Street Bridge over the blue water of False Creek and its mix of old warehouses and neat rows of townhouses. The water sparkles under the lowering sun and the city takes on shades of gold as the traffic begins to clear. I take Richards Street and then Davie before turning into the shaded alley behind the St. Helen's Hotel. After parking my car, I pull down my sleeves, put my leather jacket back on, and walk into the bar, dark and comfortable, where I see Chico sitting with Stan, a heroin dealer in his forties I had already met a couple of times playing pool in the Blackstone.

Stan is a short, toothless man with narrow shoulders and a prominent beer belly that gives him a pregnant sort of profile. A thin moustache stains his upper lip, while a mullet of curly, brown hair flows down the back of his bald head.

"Anything happening?" I ask as usual.

"Gotta watch the heat.... They're fucking everywhere," Stan says in a whiny tone, his eyes opening wide as fifty-cent pieces as he stabs his cigarette into the ashtray.

Stan likes to make things bigger than they are. This is just another day for the local cops, but he likes to talk about the heat as if he knew something no one else does.

"I heard the cops picked up a guy in the Blackstone," Chico adds.

"The fucking pigs put the boots to him. They have nothing on him," Stan continues. "That's what they do when they have nothing on you, they beat the piss out of you."

"I have a guy, works for me," I say, "They kept him for two hours in a parking lot slapping him around and trying to scare him. He never talked or nothing. He had a black eye and his eye was all red from blood and he had sore ribs, but nothing broken because they didn't want him to go to the hospital."

I like dealing with people like Stan and Chico. It's easier for me than with some of the other heroin addicts because they are criminals first and drug users second. Like Chico, Stan looks for a score wherever he can get it, and if you want to grab his attention, all you have to do is begin with "I know a guy...."

Stan nods and stares at me. "That's what I'd do, better take your lumps and keep your mouth shut."

After a while, Stan walks off to do some business. Chico and I leave St. Helen's and walk across to the Blackstone. Whenever I can, I try to have someone with me as I walk into the Blackstone. It gives people confidence to see me walking in with Chico. Ironically, of all the heroin users in the Blackstone, Chico is the only one who has seen me since the beginning, and I know that if people go to him he will tell them that he doesn't know me well enough to sell to me.

Inside the Blackstone, Captain Kangaroo is sitting with a few rounders, none of them heroin users. We sit at his table. They are watching a boxing match on a small television hanging from the ceiling. Unlike many of the other hypes, you can sit with Kangaroo and watch the Canucks play the Canadiens, or talk about Sugar Ray Leonard, Duran, or Marvelous Marvin Hagler.

After a while, Stan comes in and takes a seat against the wall. People go to him and I figure that he has scored and is dirty. A few tables over, Deedee sits by herself, on the nod. She has done morphine and is scratching her arms constantly. I want to show Stan that I am connected so I walk up to her. Deedee raises her head and aims her pinhole pupils at me.

"Hi," she says, her head bobbing slightly as she tries to focus.

"Hey Deedee, looks like there's some good stuff around."

Deedee smiles. "You're not kidding."

Deedee's eyes slowly close and her head drops down until her chin is an inch away from the beer soaked tablecloth. After a few seconds, her head moves up and she looks at me again.

"Listen Deedee, the stuff I got from you last time was pretty good. I have a friend who is looking for a B."

"You're looking for a B, I can...."

I await eagerly the end of her sentence, but Deedee closes her eyes and lets her head come down again. I sit and wait in silence, wondering if I lost her for good this time, but her head rises up again.

"...get it for you."

"I thought that you might introduce me to somebody," I say, amazed that she can maintain the thread of the conversation.

"I'll need to ..." she begins, her eyelids drooping, "...call some body, but he won't be able to do it until tomorrow. It has morphine in it."

I am always surprised by how coherent people are in between nods. Drunks will lose their train of thought and become incoherent when they pass out, but junkies don't. They just open a door inside their brains and leave the room for a few seconds.

Deedee scratches her arm.

"How much?" I ask.

"Depends, if you come and fix with me...." Her head comes down again, this time without coming back up for a while, so I decide to leave it and return to Captain Kangaroo's table. Back on my seat, I look around me and see Kitty sitting with some friends. She scratches her arm slowly from wrist to shoulder.

"That morphine makes you scratch, man," Chico says looking at Kitty.

"At least, it's clean," adds Captain Kangaroo.

"Better than the shit I get in George," I say. "The last joint I did clogged up my outfit ...had to throw it away."

"I know, I did some junk once. It was cut with rat poison, what you call it ...strychnine, yeah and after, like, I couldn't move my fingers." Chico curls his fingers as if he had claws. "I was scared. I couldn't even open the door," he continues, pretending to press his crippled hands against a doorknob to turn it.

"You gotta know what you're buying," I say.

Two Street Crew members come in and do their rounds. Sitting where I am, I can feel the hate in the silence that follows. These cops come in and spend their time between the bars of the Granville Strip as if drugs, alcohol, and crime were shoved into these bars for the police to deal with.

After the cops have gone, Chico brings his face close to mine. "Stan has some good stuff."

"I'm interested."

"If you give me money and put me into action, I'll sell it for you and we can make some money."

"I just want it for myself."

"But I don't want to sell to you. I don't know you. I'll just give you the profit from the sale, you know."

"Just ask around, people have seen me fix," I lie.

"Doesn't mean anything. I knew a narc once, he did three joints a fix."

"Forget it then. I got my own thing."

"You can trust me," Chico says, looking at me in the eyes.

"I'll see if I can scrape some coin together. But you got to be straight when you sell it. I don't want to lose my coin."

"Let me know," Chico says before leaving the bar. "You can trust me."

In a corner of the bar Stan deals a few caps to a hooker. I get up and walk out, and then make my way to the Austin, where I find Charlie sitting alone. I walk up to him.

"Anything happening?"

"Nothing, come and see me later."

When I return to the Blackstone, Stan is still sitting at his table. I walk over to him.

"You got?"

Stan leans back in his chair and looks at me straight as if I had just challenged him to a fight. "I don't got. Who told you I got?"

"Chico did."

"I don't got ...I don't fucking know you," he says in his strong nasal whine.

I should walk away, but I decide to push it.

"Chico knows me," I say. "I just want one."

Stan gets up and walks around the pool tables to a corner table filled with beer where a group of familiar faces are sitting. There, I spot Chico sitting among the group, laughing and chatting, and I know that I've been caught at my own game. Stan leans into him, talking, and Chico glances at me shaking his head.

Stan comes back to his table where I sit alone, seeing a good day's work unravel before me.

"Chico says he don't fucking know you. He's known you for just a month."

"Well, fuck him. I know him. Nothing to do with you, man. I know him good enough so I don't know why he said that."

I return to my table empty-handed and see Chico walk toward me. Before he can reach my table, Stan calls him over and they speak again, both staring at me. After a few minutes, Chico comes over, barely looking me in the eyes.

"I got it."

"What?"

"I got it. Give me the money ...give me the money."

I pull thirty-five dollars out of the inside of my boot and give it to him. Chico holds his closed hand towards me. I pull a piece of tinfoil out of my shirt pocket and he drops a small red and white cap into it. With his record, it's enough to send Chico back to jail. I wrap the cap and place it inside my mouth.

"It's apple juice," he says despondently. "Don't forget to add citric acid to it from a lemon or something so it doesn't jam your outfit."

"Thanks."

"You owe me."

Chico walks back to Stan and gives him the money.

I walk out of the bar and come across Charlie who is on his way to the Blackstone, looking morose and pensive. He is a big man and his Fu Manchu gives him a tough look, but he is gentle and friendly.

"How's it going?" I ask.

"You seen my girlfriend?"

"Who's your girlfriend?"

"You know, Amy."

"Didn't know you guys were together ...haven't seen her."

Amy is a young, pretty girl. I have a hard time picturing her with old man Charlie, but she's one of our targets and a heavy user, and, as plain and dull as Charlie is, he has lots of connections.

"Hey, you know Stan, don't you?" I ask.

"I know him."

"Can I trust him?"

"Yeah, you can trust him. He's a little cagey, but you can trust him. Why? Has he got?"

"Yeah, but I don't know if his stuff is good."

"Well, you can come and see me later if you need anything."

"Okay. I'll see how it goes."

"I'll be here," Charlie says without looking at me, his large bare forehead and quiet manner injecting an aura of authority into his few words.

Satisfied that at least I have Charlie on my side, I keep on walking and leave the Strip, wondering how long I can keep this up.

WHO'S GOT?

I want to keep out of trouble, but sometimes trouble finds you wherever you are, and you can't do anything about it. In the past few days, I kept a low profile, but Chico is staying close to me, pushing for me to put him into action so he can convince himself that I'm not a cop. I keep him waiting by inventing one excuse or another, but he stays with me, watching, and trying to decide if he will make good money with me, or else go to jail. My job is to keep buying heroin from people I still haven't bought from, but with Chico at my side and unwilling to vouch for me, it's getting complicated.

Chico and I sit at the small row of tables against the wall when Captain Kangaroo comes in and takes a seat at the table next to ours.

"How's it going?" I ask.

"Good," he says.

Captain Kangaroo stares ahead. On that day, he is the Man and people come to him to score. I haven't bought from him yet, but I feel good about going to him. I just don't want to hit him up with Chico at my side.

"Let's go to the Austin," I tell Chico.

"When are you going back to Prince George," he asks.

"I'm thinking about going next week."

We walk into the Austin and find the Street Crew shaking somebody down. We keep on walking and head out to Jerry's Café.

"Want something?"

"Yeah, sure, lets get some chicken."

I buy the fried chicken and we take a seat at one of the booths.

"I can go with you to George if you want. I can do some of the driving," Chico says, chewing on a chicken leg.

"It's better if I do it myself. I'm doing good, and I don't want any heat when I go up there. If you fix me with a connection, maybe we can do something."

"Not unless I do it myself. If you're a cop and I introduce you to somebody I'm finished."

"Shit, man, you know I'm not a cop. You saw me on the nod and all. Maybe we can go and fix together sometime."

"Like I told you, I knew a cop who was a junkie."

Since Chico sold to me, the word "cop" floats in the air between the two of us just about every time we talk business. He rips a piece of fried skin with his fingers and lets it drop into his mouth. "Be careful with who you do business up there," he mumbles.

"My people are solid."

"You don't have to go all the way to Prince George, man. I can do it all for you right here."

I put my food down and look at him. "I know you can, Chico. I know you're solid and all ...but this place is too fucking hot and the cops know you. I'm new in town and I want to keep a low profile. I have a girl in Burnaby and she doesn't even know what I do. She works for the government, at the driver's licence office. If I'm careful, I've got it made."

Chico sucks the fat off his fingers. "She a user?"

"No, not really. Sometimes we share a cap, but I have to be careful with her. She gets sick easy."

When we return to the Blackstone I find a seat near Kangaroo's table, next to Pedophile Palmer.

"You gonna be around later?" I ask Chico to let him know that I have things to do that don't involve him.

"Sure," he says throwing a glance around the table.

Chico walks off to play pool.

Palmer is a loner. He and I never speak much, but sitting with the Kangaroo Man makes me popular and Palmer asks how I am.

"The heat's out at the Austin," I say. "The tall one with the short stocky guy ...they were giving somebody a hard time."

"They'll be here soon," he says, licking his thin lips. The skin on his face is waxy and colourless, and his blue eyes keep moving nervously under the shadow of his black cowboy hat.

"There's gonna be some good stuff later," he adds, as if we're now a team. He leans in. "Kangaroo has some okay stuff, but it's not great."

I nod. The cover team told me that the streets are dry, with the purity hovering around one to two per cent.

Cindy comes in with a young Asian girl and, after throwing me a short glance, sits with her friend at our joined tables. Her voice is hoarse and the straight lines of her jaw give her a hint of toughness that presents a stark contrast to her small frame and pretty blue eyes. The same toughness she showed me a couple of months before, when she ripped me off.

Cindy looks me over before turning to Captain Kangaroo. "You know him?" she asks, nodding in my direction.

"Yeah, but I can't vouch for him," says Kangaroo.

"Ever fixed with him?"

"He's all right. But I can't vouch for him."

Cindy looks at me suspiciously between drags of cigarette

smoke. Many of the hypes in the Blackstone talk to the police in some way or another, and the only people junkies can really trust are doing time either in Oakalla or the BC Pen.

Cindy looks sick so she doesn't let her concerns about me or anyone else get in her way. She turns to Captain Kangaroo. "You got?"

The Captain nods.

Cindy looks at her friend. "You want one, right? It's your first one so I don't want you to do more than one."

The girl shrugs. She lights up a cigarette and turns her head to the side to blow a cloud of smoke. She's not yet bruised by the streets and has the cockiness of a youth taking on the world. I look at the junkies around me, Captain Kangaroo, Cindy, Chico, and Palmer. It's hard to imagine them sitting together anywhere else. A strange mix of old and young, street thugs and clever operators all caught up in the daily struggles of the street. A few tables over I see Charlie, a nice guy who, well into his forties, still wears the jeans and black leather jacket he could have worn in high school, when smoking grass behind the fence was the highlight of his day. Amy is now sitting with him. The cute prom queen and the old pothead. Together, they don't fight the appeal of drugs anymore than the drunks of the Blackstone fight alcoholism. None of the users do. Further down, the Accountant enjoys a beer in his dress shirt and V-neck sweater. There are the trans women, who seem to feel at home in a place that holds no prejudice, and the young, pretty girls who, like Amy, are loved by many, but love drugs more than anything else.

"I want four," Cindy says, slipping Kangaroo $140 under the table. Kangaroo spits the bundle into his hand and works on the knot when the two cops walk in through the front door, their eyes fixed on our row of tables.

"Six!" I say under my breath.

The Captain tightens up. The two cops stroll over.

"Captain Kangaroo," says the tall one with a smile.

The old man smiles. "Good afternoon."

I can tell by the steadiness of his stare that fear had a grasp of his insides, but he keeps on a friendly face.

"It's real quiet today, isn't it?" Cindy says to the cops, herself motivated by the fear of losing her cash and only chance to score.

The cop smiles at her. "I don't know.... Is it, Cindy?"

"Yeah. Everybody's being good," she answers in her raspy voice.

The cop looks at me. "Who's your friend?"

"You tell me. Don't know him."

"What's your name?"

"Nick."

"Where you from, Nick?"

"Burnaby."

The other cop looks me over, but doesn't say a word and I wonder if he's guessed who I really am. I'm sure the word got around among the local street cops that we have an operation going, even if no one knows who the operator is.

"Got ID, Nick?"

I give the cop my driver's licence.

"Let's see your arms," he says after having passed the ID to his companion.

"Here?" I ask.

Cindy turns and glares at me. "Show them your fucking arms!" her eyes are saying.

"We can go outside, if you want," the cop says.

I roll up my sleeves. The cop looks at the tracks on my arms then reads my face for a second before giving me back my ID.

"Who's got, Captain?" the cop asks.

Kangaroo looks away. He has been around long enough to know that if he weren't a slight bit cocky it wouldn't be right.

"Beats me."

The cop is standing within arm's reach of Kangaroo's throat.

I can tell that he's thinking about taking the old man down. Cindy's friend seems to be missing the point, blowing smoke away as if it didn't have anything to do with her.

"Hi, boys!" interrupts Deedee. She flops her lean body on a chair, looking at the cop with a flirty smile. "Looking for a little fun?"

"Stay clean," the cop says to the table before walking away.

Somehow, Deedee seems to operate on a different plane than the rest of the junkies.

"I know the one cop, he's all right," she says.

Cindy watches the cops leaving the bar through the back door, the hate on her face flickering with every heartbeat.

"I can get juice if anyone's interested," Deedee announces.

"I don't like methadone," Cindy snaps without looking at her.

"The price is right...."

Kangaroo passes the four caps to Cindy under the table. She wraps them and gives them to her friend, who slips the package into her pants. They leave without saying a word.

The waiter comes to the table and Deedee orders some more beers. Soon, the Accountant moves in and sits beside me. He leans ahead and put his hands together between his thighs, staring through his horn-rimmed glasses at the few beers sitting on the table.

"May I have one of these beers?" he asks in a strong British accent.

"Sure, go ahead," I say.

Further down on dealer's row, Charlie's big bare forehead shines in the light as he talks to a customer. It's good that he sees me at Captain Kangaroo's table. Now that I sit with them, the dealers have to decide for themselves where I fit in. I am gaining the trust of both Deedee and the Captain and it begins to rub off on the others.

Later on, Harry and Maggie come in and sit with us. Maggie has just come back from turning tricks and her hand squeezes a roll of bills, which she gives to Harry. He counts the bills and orders some beer.

I look around me and it's as if all the pictures pinned to the wall of the Shack have come to life.

By the time Jimmy and Selina come in, less than an hour later, all I need to do is sit back. Jimmy shakes his umbrella, spraying water all around him, and places it under his chair, next to me.

"How is it going?" I ask.

"Fucking rain."

"Grab a beer."

He and I got along from the first day I met him. Jimmy is always on the move, so we usually just say hi and chat a bit before he moves on, the bald eagle on the back of his jacket floating over the bar. We get along because he's a hustler who lives by the code of the street. With him, it isn't about the heroin. It's about the business of crime and hustling scores, and as a cop I can relate to that. We understand each other without saying too much, and from a street perspective there is already some level of mutual respect.

Jimmy keeps his jacket on while his girlfriend Selina takes off her knee-length leather coat and drapes it carefully over the back of her chair. Her chiselled, dark features and Afro make her stand out on the street where she stands alongside Maggie on most nights. When I see them turn tricks, on my way to the Blackstone, I can tell that she and Maggie look out for each other.

A girl comes in and, without a word, sits at our table. She is pretty, if not beautiful, clean and young, and her skin fresh. Full, dark hair frames her face and a gold bracelet wraps her small white wrist.

She turns to Selina. "I need Vs."

"I'll be back in a second."

The girl opens her designer purse and paints her lips. She wears expensive clothes and little makeup. She doesn't fit in, but no one pays attention.

Selina comes back with Kitty.

"They're fifty each, how many do you want?" Kitty asks, pulling a chair.

"Six."

"Okay, that's about ...let see ...times fifty ...fifty's a hard number to multiply, not easy like thirty-five."

Kitty looks at me, but I can't tell if she's joking.

"Okay, that's three dollars."

The girl gives her the money and pops in two of the Valium. I don't know what demons she is appeasing with the Valium. She picks up my beer and chases the pills down with it, before walking away without a word, leaving nothing behind, but a red lipstick stain and the strong smell of perfume on my beer glass.

The bar is filling up and on the large speakers at each end of the room David Bowie invites people to dance. I listen to the music and get into the groove of the moment. Over at the pool tables, Chico seems to be doing well because he's been holding on to his table for several games.

Jimmy sits with his back straight and looks in front of him. He is intimidating and knows it. People often come to him to chat, laugh, or to talk seriously about a problem they have. Sometimes, they'll whisper in his ear and draw a snicker from him.

"Where do you live?" Jimmy asks.

"I've got a place in Burnaby, but it's temporary," I say. "I'm thinking of moving closer to here. There's nothing for me in Burnaby."

"What the fuck is here, man? There's fuck-all here."

"It's a good place if you know the right people."

"You gotta be careful around here. If you need anything, let me know. I know a lot of people around here."

Jimmy finishes his beer.

"We're gonna go eat, you want to come?"

"No, I gotta stay. I'm looking for somebody."

I'm happy to leave things where they are with Jimmy, and to

show him that I don't need anything from him. He looks like a guy who could take me to a new supplier and I know that I'll see him again soon. It's a street operation, but we all want to go up the chain and catch a bigger fish. It's the nature of police work. Get a bigger case, more drugs in the locker, and more jail time for the target. It's in the back of my mind every time I walk into the Blackstone.

I sit with the Accountant for a while, both our backs to the wall, with our eyes on the action. He likes both heroin and hookers, and when a known user named Frank comes in with two girls, he waves them over to our table and before long they are pooling their money together. The Accountant stares at the girls' skinny legs every time they move around, and it's difficult to tell whether the girls or the heroin are more important to him. Frank tells Captain Kangaroo that he and the Accountant want eight caps, and I figured that it's a good opportunity for me to score from the Captain without bringing too much attention. I give the thirty-five dollars to Frank and he puts it together with the other bills before passing the money to Captain Kangaroo.

"That's nine," Frank says to Kangaroo without hesitating.

When Frank gets the heroin, he and the Accountant get ready to leave with the girls.

"I want my cap," I say to him.

Everyone stops and looks at me.

"You're coming with us, aren't you?" Frank says. "We're all going to the same place."

"No, sorry man, I gotta go to Burnaby."

The table chills and Frank exchanges looks with the others. The Accountant and the girls just stare at me. I miscalculated again. For them, leaving all together is the surest way to ensure that no one in the group will talk to the cops. I feel their eyes on me; feel the heat again. Kitty is silent, probably thinking of the time she sold to me.

"I really have to go," I say. "I have people waiting for me."

Frank looks around him. He spits the balloon into his hand and unties the knot. There is nothing worse for a hype than handling the material after a score. The idea is to get out to a safe place before anything can happen. I can see the irritation in his face as he drops the cap into my open hand.

I pick up a piece of tinfoil from an empty cigarette package sitting on the table and wrap the cap carefully before putting it into my mouth. Frank and his group walk out of the Blackstone without saying anything, the anticipation of the fix overtaking any other thought. I follow them out to the corner of Granville and Davie Streets. Frank, the Accountant, and the hookers cross Davie while I wait for my light to turn. That's when I hear a car screech to a stop.

Across the street, the Accountant and the two girls are staring at the ground behind the cop car. I can no longer see Frank, but can see two cops bend over him, struggling. Frank has been jumped and before long he is standing with his hands behind his back. One of the cops is busy putting something into a plastic bag so I know that he wasn't able to swallow the drugs in time. The other hypes look on, the anticipation of the fix vanishing. I keep on walking and hope that no one is looking at me. Maybe the two cops who came into the bar have figured out that some action was going to happen and have arranged for the Street Crew to jump Frank. I don't believe that Chico and Captain Kangaroo are informants. Regardless, this is bad luck and I know that the heat will get back to me again one way or another.

PEOPLE ARE SAYING THINGS ABOUT YOU

An advantage of working a bar in the city, unlike small towns, is that no one ever has the full picture. I know that people have talked about me, and are wondering how it is that I walked away free only a few metres from where Frank was jumped by the cops. He is still in jail, so I don't have to worry about him, but his friends have lost their dope and money and likely spent the night sick, while I kept both my smack and my freedom. This is just bad luck, but on the bright side the only person who has a good reason to get back at me is Frank, and he is out of the game. It's up to me to fix things with the others.

Once inside the Blackstone, a short glance from Kitty makes me feel uneasy. The kind of glance that connects with you eye-to-eye and then shuts you down even before you get started. I look around and see a few familiar faces, but no one offers me the kind of look that invites you to join in, only the heavy quietness of their cold shoulder. At the far end of the bar two uniforms chat while looking over the action—like prison guards in a crowded jail—but there is no heroin around so the hypes don't pay attention to them.

The Accountant and Crowley exchange a word when they see me, and I begin to feel like a lame animal trying to join the herd. With all my activity as an undercover cop it's ironic that I am getting heat for something that has nothing to do with me. But here I am, and anything can set them off against me. To make the obvious official, Chico walks up to me before I can find a seat. He is wearing a greasy mackinaw and his white running shoes have lost their shine. He brings his face close to mine and I smell the sweat in his beard.

"Be careful...people are saying things about you," he says quietly.

He walks out and leaves me to ponder his words, wondering if they were a threat or a friendly heads-up. I go directly to Captain Kangaroo's table and take a seat next to him with my back to the wall. He keeps looking straight ahead.

"Pretty dry isn't it," I say.

Kangaroo keeps looking ahead.

"There's nothing around," I add.

A nod.

"You heard what happened to Frank?" I ask.

"Yeah," he says, still looking ahead.

"I was there. I was walking out with him and a few guys when I heard some tires screeching. Then Frank was down on the ground."

We both stared ahead, side by side.

"They hang out together after a score," I continue, "just draw the heat. Somebody ratted him out ...they knew ...they never even touched the others. Never touched me ...and that shit wasn't even good."

Captain Kangaroo looks at me for the first time, scrutinizing. The heroin came from him and I might have insulted him, but he knows that it wasn't good and I need to be upfront about it. I don't want to leave the Blackstone without saying my piece, but I don't want to overdo it. Nothing is tougher than defending yourself against a lie; you try too hard and you sink deeper, like trying to fight your way out of quicksand.

"These guys ...they bring the heat ...getting together to fix. I'm glad I fucking stayed away. They're the ones who bring the heat. I'm fucking glad I didn't go with them."

Captain Kangaroo looks at me. "Yeah, I don't like these groupie fixes either."

All I can do now is hope that Captain Kangaroo will take my side when I am not there. I order more beer, and after a while, two hookers come in and argue with Crowley about some bad heroin he sold them. The Blackstone is dry, any available heroin has been cut to nothing with milk sugar, and the bad stuff is beginning to irritate the nerves of most three-cap addicts.

"I know! It's all shit," Crowley repeats emphatically to the hookers, shrugging his shoulders like a salesman unwilling to provide a refund.

"That's all there is, shit!" he continues.

Crowley slides his wiry frame onto a chair next to the Captain. The heroin has stripped his body of its fat, leaving nothing but muscle and sinew. Somehow, except for the yellow tinge of his skin, being a heroin addict works for him.

"I did six caps this morning, but didn't feel a thing," he says to Captain Kangaroo in frustration.

"Somebody's gonna get hurt," I throw in, without looking at them.

Crowley gives me a look and his pale blue eyes try to figure me out.

"Fucking right somebody's gonna get hurt," he says after a beat. "Now they even come from the Skids trying to sell this shit. This isn't the fucking Skids! This guy, he had shit in a fucking paper and wanted sixty for it. There was nothing in it, you know. You could tell just by looking at it ...but somebody bought it. Somebody's gonna get shanked."

I can feel the tension loosen around me as I sit and chat with

Captain Kangaroo and Crowley. Other users come in and the attention turns to them. Violence is around, but no longer on me. It is now on the bad stuff going around. In the Blackstone, violence is always on people's minds, but there are too many things to lash out at so they wait and see what will land in front of them, like lizards in a box full of crickets.

The next day, I sit alone, pretending that I'm on the nod. The day after that, I sit with Deedee and sell her a clean outfit for two dollars. "I left it in the girls' washroom behind the tank if you need it," she says with a smile, her pupils already pin points. Crowley is sitting next to her holding a bundle in his mouth. People come in and score from him and chat with Deedee and me while he sorts out the heroin. I stay away from the action—just being there is enough—and hope no one gets jumped.

Frank hasn't come back to the Blackstone and is probably still in jail going cold turkey. This is good for me. Even if he is out, a court order will have him stay away from the Granville Strip and that is also good for me. If he comes back, he'll bring the heat on me again, but for now people are slowly forgetting, their attention going to their own sickness, to the cops always watching, and to the people who rip them off. Out of pure bad luck my credibility has been damaged, but there is more than enough heat to go around. I just have to make sure not to bring it on me again for a while.

When the action comes back, a few days later, it comes in full force with ten per cent white heroin flooding the streets again. Everyone is getting connected, and except for a few hypes dying of overdoses, the Blackstone becomes a beehive of activity. There's heroin and I have money. On the street, nothing else matters, and anything that happened before has been forgotten. It is just a matter of time before I find someone connected to this new source of heroin.

When I see Chico walk towards me again I worry that he will make things difficult for me, but then I see that he has a web of deep cuts on his bare forehead, something he likely got from a broken bottle. The cuts are glistening, wet, and fresh.

"Do you have a gun?" he asks.

"No, I don't have a gun."

"I want to fucking kill someone," he says.

"I don't have a gun."

"Fuck! I need something.... Can you get me a cap?"

"I have nothing."

"I have a fucking headache."

"No kidding," I say, looking at the fresh oozing cuts on his receding hairline.

Chico drifts away to look for Kitty. He buys Valium and I watch him walk out of the bar, alone. He looks down and out with his damaged head, his missing teeth, his greasy clothes, and his messy beard. And I feel a lot stronger.

JIMMY AND THE BIG LEAGUES

A few days later, I sit alone and see Harry come down with his old lady Maggie. Harry scans the bar and we make eye contact. There is no one else around and it works for me because he walks over. I throw some money on the table and we shake hands.

"How is it going," I ask.

Harry and Maggie sit down and Red immediately comes over to drop a half dozen glasses of beer on the table. Harry reaches for a glass and takes a couple of hearty swigs.

"Do you live in town?" I ask.

"Yeah, we're in town."

"I'm looking for a place."

"There's lots of rooms around here, pretty cheap too. Plus you don't need a car if you live here."

"I need my car. I have to go up north once in a while."

"What do you do there?"

"I know some people there in the construction business. I'm a roofer so they call me when they need somebody. They pay my gas and everything."

Maggie takes a sip of beer and sinks back into her chair. "Nice. You must be good at it," she says with a smirk.

"When I do something I do it right," I say returning the smile. "You gotta do it right if you want something out of it."

"Like everything else," Harry adds.

Jimmy comes in and sees Harry. He gives me a tap on the shoulder and takes a seat next to him. Jimmy and Harry have their own thing going, each a drug addict relying on his girlfriend to work the street and bring in the cash. When they are alone with the girls, I see couples who deal with their addiction together. But when the guys are together, the women don't seem to count. The guys run the business and their job is to protect that business. They may be drug addicts, but they are street criminals first and for me it's a nice change, working with crime instead of addiction. That's what I'm here for. I can talk to them about anything that brings in money, as long as it's illegal.

"How's it going?" Jimmy asks.

"I need to do a run up north and make some money, but I gotta get my car fixed first."

"What's wrong with it?"

"I was driving on Kingsway ...right in the middle of Kingsway ...and the hood flew open. Hit me right in the windshield, couldn't see anything."

Harry laughs. "That's funny."

"It's not funny," Maggie says. "He could have got hurt."

"Didn't break the windshield or nothing, but I have to tie the hood down. Maybe it's time to get a new car. I don't want to have the bulls on me going to George. Takes me ten hours if I go direct. Just stop for gas and a piss. Do you know how much it costs to buy a cap over there?"

"I know," says Jimmy. "I've been there. Fifty bucks a cap. You can't get good heroin in George. You're lucky if you get one per cent."

Jimmy takes a sip from one of the two glasses of beer Red dropped in front of him. He looks out at the people coming in.

"I know this guy, he has a .357, still in the grease," he says to Harry, "never been fired."

"I'm fucking broke, man."

"You waste too much time selling single caps. If you get some money together, I can hook you up for bundles."

Harry and Jimmy keep on talking about heroin, but I'm not in the conversation so I lean back and look around me. A guy comes by our table and stands around.

"How's it going?" I ask.

"Good."

"Sit down, man, you make me nervous."

The man sits down next to me. He says he's in Pemberton planting trees.

"That's fucking hard work, man. Here, have a beer."

"Yeah, it's okay. I'm just here to relax ...taking it easy, you know. But I don't know anybody."

"What you looking for?" I ask.

"I want to score a couple caps of heroin. Somebody told me to come here."

"Sorry, man, I don't fucking know you," I say.

I turn to Jimmy. "Do you know this guy?"

"Never seen him."

"Wants a couple joints of heroin."

Jimmy leans forward and stares at the man.

"Get out of this fucking bar, you fucking narc, and don't fucking come back."

He looks at him as if he is dirt and I can tell that he feels good doing it. The guy stands up. He has a mix of fear and anger on his puzzled face and doesn't want to let go.

"I just want to score a couple caps, just for myself," he says.

"Get the fuck out!" Jimmy says.

"Go back to your police car," Harry throws in for good measure.

Jimmy stands up and gets in the guy's face. The guy looks at me for a moment and then turns around and walks away. Jimmy sits down. He is pumped and still has his game face on. If you want to do well on the street, someone else has to be lower than you.

"The money's in bundles," he says again, but to me this time. "You don't make anything selling caps, so you need people working for you. I had a great dealer working for me, but he went back to Montréal after I went in the joint."

"How long were you in for," I ask.

"I did four years."

Selina walks in from the streets and smiles at me before planting a kiss on Jimmy's lips. She gives him a roll of money.

"Traffic was good today," she says.

Jimmy stuffs the money in his pocket, smiles, and pulls a chair out for her.

"Let's go out tonight for dinner. I feel like a steak."

I see a girl walk in. Her face has been cut all over. Unlike the mess you get from a broken windshield, these are long, clean cuts. She has stitches around her cheeks, forehead, and chin. Long vicious cuts. I feel like bringing it up, but no one else seems to care. She's a regular, a hustler, and I see her regularly hopping from one table to another. Even with all the fresh stitches, she is cheery and walks and talks like any other day. No one pays attention to the cuts on her face.

"Nick, you coming for dinner with us?" asks Jimmy.

"No, thanks, I'm gonna hang around here for a while. I'm trying to collect money from somebody."

"If you need help collecting, let me know. I take a third."

"Good, I might take you up on that."

"Let me know. A third might be a lot for you, but it's better than losing the whole thing."

Cindy walks in and comes to our table. She has become a

barometer of sorts that lets me know how I am doing. She was quick to spot me as a mark when we first met, and she was nervous around me for a while, but she has loosened up since. She's a street animal driven by instinct, and now that she comes directly to my table, I know that I'm making progress. She stands with one knee on a chair and takes a deep drag from her cigarette.

"Is there anything around?" she asks Jimmy in her gravely voice.

"Nothing," Jimmy says without looking at her.

We all watch Cindy walk away.

"I heard that her old man just got out of the joint," Harry says.

"Yeah, he was around earlier. Got to watch them when they're together," Jimmy says. "They'll fuck you up if they can."

After giving Cindy the cold shoulder, we sit quietly, comfortable in owning our table.

"How much is that piece?" I ask Jimmy.

"You interested?"

"Yeah, I need something for when I go out of town." With nothing else going I might as well take a gun off the street.

"Four hundred, in the grease."

"It's a lot of money, but I'll take a look at it," I say.

A DAY WITH JIMMY

Jimmy has impeccably trimmed, curly hair, a well-kept goatee, and every day he wears his tan leather jacket with the large eagle spread out on the back. He makes the Blackstone his home, and people are used to the eagle coasting among its tables, watching over Selina while she works the street.

We have been hanging around together for a few days already, becoming friends. We both look for the big score and see an opportunity in each other's company, even if we don't yet know what it is. When Jimmy walks in and sees me, he walks over, and I look for him whenever I come in. Unlike Chico, who knows his place and sticks to what's in front of him, Jimmy has ambitions. Granville Street is his place of business. With his wife's street work paying the bills, he can afford to sit in the bar and look for bigger scores.

Everyone knows that I have business in Prince George, but no one knows exactly what it is. My job is to give just enough information for them to figure out that I am up to something. First, I don't want to be too specific, because it's easier to let people figure things out themselves, and second, I can adjust my story to fit whatever situation or opportunity presents itself. If I have a deal going, I let Jimmy know, telling him that I have things to do. And then I let him know that I need to do a quick run to Prince George. Jimmy fills the blanks; he's good at that. The most important thing for me is that I look busy. It's the only thing I have to protect myself. People don't know how connected I am, or how far I'm willing to go if things don't turn out the way I want. So I walk around and throw in just enough information to keep them thinking that there is more to me than what they know.

Jimmy and I usually meet first in the Blackstone and then walk across the street to the Austin, each looking for people we know and see if there is anything we can get into. If there's nothing happening at the Austin, we move on and stop by the Theodore and then back to the Blackstone.

"I'm looking, but there's nothing around," I tell Jimmy on one night.

"I don't know who's got," he says. "Me and Selina ...we do 'Talwin.'"

"I never tried them?"

"I used to do H, but I don't touch it now. Ts are clean and they keep us steady, no highs and lows."

Jimmy doesn't talk much about his drug use. It's part of his life and it doesn't have anything to do with his daily business. I take the same approach with him, keeping my habit to myself. This complicity, along with our talk of scores and our hanging out together, always looking for something to happen, is building into a friendship. Every time he and I stop somewhere, I go to work and try to figure out if there's anything I can get into. It gives Jimmy confidence that I have been around long enough to know people and talk heroin with them, but I never get Jimmy fully into my business. He keeps his distance whenever I talk business with someone, and if I score heroin, I just leave the bar without a word to him. It also gives people confidence to see that we get along. Street crime is his life. Sometimes, when Selina feels threatened by a john or anyone else on her corner, Jimmy will emerge from the Blackstone with a couple of guys to fix things. Other than that, his job is to cruise the bar and sit there while his girlfriend works the street, alone on her corner at Granville and Helmcken, waiting for some stranger to pick her up in his car. Jimmy hangs around the bars until she is done, the eagle gliding from the Blackstone to the Austin, and then to Theo's, always looking for a score. Selina never comes back without the trick money and he is willing to sit patiently and drink beer until she shows up with it. Once he has the money, Jimmy goes to the Skids and picks up the Ts. Talwin comes in the form of yellow, commercial tablets and they sell on the Skids for seven dollars apiece. They need seven of them for each fix, twice a day, every day, but I never see them on the nod. When he is back, they walk together to their apartment on Davie Street, a small one-bedroom on the second floor, and fix together.

Jimmy and I are sitting together when Selina walks up to our table and gives her man a kiss, passing money into his hand. She is pretty and her eyes threw daggers at me the day I asked if she was East Indian.

"I'm from Fiji!" she said.

"Sorry."

Jimmy stands up, ready to leave. "Still interested in the piece?"

"I want to look at it first," I say.

"We can go now if you want. I need to see him."

"Let's take my car."

Jimmy and I leave Selina in the bar and walk across Granville Street. There is something ungiving about him, like a stiff wire that would rather break than bend. His clean jeans, resting neatly on heeled boots, give added height to his already imposing stature, and his steady pace, leaning slightly forward, gives the impression that he would back away from no one. We arrive to the parking lot behind Theo's where my beat-up yellow Datsun 510 is waiting for us, its hood bent and tied down with a thick cord.

"The guy is serious. I don't know if he'll want to talk with you," Jimmy says as soon as we get in.

"Yeah, no problem."

"If you want to try it, I can take you somewhere."

"Sure. No rush. I don't have a job for it. I'm getting into some shit right now so I just want it around."

We start our drive to the Skids.

The bar is empty when we walk in. In a corner, three men sit at the only occupied table and stare at us. One of them stands and walks over behind the bar. Tiny is six-foot-four and must weigh over 250 pounds.

"How's Selina?" he asks Jimmy.

"She's good."

"She's a doll. Sweet girl you got. Have you seen Spanky?"

"No. Haven't seen Spanky since before he went to the joint."

"These fucking guys come out of the joint and you help them and they fuck with you. I said I can help the guy ...comes out all hyper and wants to work and then he fucks with my stuff."

Tiny picks up a plastic bag from behind the counter and gives it to Jimmy. After having put the money away, he leans forward in a friendly way, his tattooed forearms resting against the bar.

"In good shape, though. Did you see him? Looks like a brick shithouse. Must have spent all his time in the joint working out."

"I didn't even know he was out," says Jimmy.

"I hear he's back with Cindy. Next time you see him tell him I'm looking for him."

Jimmy tells Tiny that I am interested in the gun. Tiny looks at me from head to toe as if he just realized that I am here.

"I don't have it here. Come back tomorrow."

The front door opens, splashing a puddle of light on the wooden floor. A couple of drunks walk in and can barely stand.

"Fuck!"

With that, Tiny quickly moves around the bar to see them out. Tiny's bar is well kept and doesn't look like a regular Skids bar. When you enter, there is no smell of stale beer and sweat to welcome you.

"Come and see me later," Tiny says to Jimmy.

When we return to the Blackstone, Selina is sitting with Harry and Maggie. Further down against the wall, Cindy sits at a table next to a big, tall, good-looking guy with an impressive build. He wears nice clothes and a trimmed moustache. They are sitting side-by-side and alone, with their backs to the wall.

"Is that Cindy's old man?" I ask.

"I don't want to talk to him. You stay away from them, they're both fucking nuts and they'll do you. Tiny can collect his own fucking money."

Spanky is tall and lean, but thick in the shoulders and neck, the way bodybuilders get when they don't like to do legwork. He looks clean and healthy, no jail tattoos, black leather jacket, or muscle shirt, just a clean open collar shirt and blue jeans. Like most of the worst head cases I've come across doing police work, he doesn't advertise the violence and wickedness he has inside.

"You'll be around later?" asks Jimmy as I stand up.

"Yeah, I'll be in."

A BAD MIX

Jimmy is deep in thought. He takes a sip of beer then leans toward me. His face is so serious that I feel like breaking into a laugh.

"For that job you told me about, I can get you what you need," he says. "A .38. Better than the .357. You just throw it away when you're done."

"Yeah, okay."

"And if you need me for something, let me know."

The job I told him about ...there is no job. It's something I made up for colour, just to keep things going with him, some "fuck-up" that I may need to fix, nothing more. I hadn't even thought out the story beyond that. Everyone tells stories on the street, most of it to impress, some of it true. The nice thing about street crime is that I don't have to say much. I shared something with him and he appreciates it. In return, he doesn't ask questions, sticking to the street code with its proud, but dumb mentality. He gave me the look that says, "Say no more, I understand."

Now he wants in without even knowing what it's about. On

top of that, he is giving me advice on how to do it and is willing to get me the gun I need. He is even ready to come with me and help. Maybe rough up somebody. I try to imagine us facing some poor soul and him showing me how it's done. Both of us going into a frenzy, our friendship solidified by a common purpose, feeling brave and tough. It could happen. It does happen. My drug team once worked on a couple of heroin traffickers who had been selling bundles and quarter ounces. Some hard case offered them some money to kill his wife and they took the contract. They drove to a quiet village on Vancouver Island, got into the house, and shot the woman. They were picked up on that same night. Two tough, stupid guys. I remember one of them staring at me as he was being booked in. He looked me in the eyes, tough and threatening. He was a strong guy, did push-ups during the whole interrogation, and, if we were both on the street, I would have been afraid. But we put him in jail for life and I went home that afternoon, had supper, and didn't think much about it after that.

Then there was this guy, about twenty years of age, clean. He had been talking with his friends about this East Indian man who had made advances to one of the white girls in the group. He never killed anyone, had never been arrested. Racism and fear fed their late night talks and one night, he quietly stood behind the guy and strangled him with a coat hanger. "You know, it's hard to kill a man," he told me, as if he was talking about moving a piano. Even in jail, with his adult life already over and an innocent man dead, the stupidity of it all hadn't yet sunk in.

That's how it starts on the street and that's how it ends. It goes from nothing and ends with nothing. From a bad idea, to a guy left in a dumpster with a few bruises and maybe a bullet or two in his body. Usually for only a few bucks, or no solid reason at all, other than this understanding that there is honour in hurting someone. Cops see it happen time and time again, and when they trace the story back, they learn that it all started with a couple of guys talking just as Jimmy and I did. The thought of violence alone is bringing Jimmy and me together. A simple thought that leads nowhere. We often glorify violence, but rarely highlight the stupidity of it.

"I'll let you know," I tell Jimmy.

We haven't even talked about what he wants in return.

MAX

Red comes to the table and unloads a few beers from a full tray that makes the sinew of his skinny forearm bulge out. Sweat is beading on his forehead, and the front part of his red hair, usually greased back, has come undone and hangs in front of his face like the bait of an anglerfish.

Jimmy pays for the beer while Selina gives a few comb strokes to her Afro. Like anyone leaving for work, she is thinking ahead and her attention has already left the table. She grabs her umbrella and puts on her long green leather coat before giving her man a kiss and walking away. Selina looks happy, and after a few steps, she looks back and waves, taking Jimmy's loving eyes and bright smile with her to her dark and rainy corner. I wonder what Jimmy is thinking ...and then not. I mean, he is not thinking, but only posturing, his face turning serious after she has gone, showing me and everyone else that he is the Man. He leans back in his chair, all business. We both take a sip of beer. The boyfriend is now a pimp.

I have dealt with hookers before and never thought much about it. To me, it is just another facet of crime. But I have already shared a few late night meals and some pretty normal conversations with Jimmy and Selina. She handles her work the same way anyone else handles a day's work. She is often happy when she is back, sometimes tired, especially after a rainy, cold day. She earns the money that pays for the rent and the drugs, while Jimmy sits comfortably in the Blackstone, ready to bring on the muscle if something goes wrong.

I look around me. The bar is filling up and my attention turns to the two tables that are connected to ours. A girl named Jodie sits quietly and smiles at me while Scotty jokes around loudly. Charlie laughs with him, his drooping moustache hanging below his creased face and balding head. I dealt with Jodie for the first time at the Austin a few days earlier, when she had some good heroin for sale. The cover team had told me that there was a spike in the heroin purity going around the Blackstone and that a few careless users had overdosed. Jodie's heroin turned out to be exactly nine per cent and she warned me to be careful when she sold it to me.

Jodie is a wholesome girl with a pretty face marked by a small scar down the corner of her left eye. She is one of these hypes who seem to maintain a normal and healthy appearance despite a strong habit. We got along immediately. Aside from the heroin use and dealing, I liked her and she seemed to like me.

"I'm trying to get off heroin," she once told me after announcing that she was on the methadone program. A few days later it bothered me to see her offering the juice for sale so she could score heroin. When you spend this much time with a group of people, relationships count no matter the type of business you're in, and for better or worse, the same goes for any long-term undercover job. Jodie is a true addict, but she treats everyone with kindness. To her, like the other heavy users in the Blackstone, the heroin highs are as good as the withdrawals are bad. She doesn't hustle anyone and keeps her deals private. She is fully functional and it makes me wonder how some people can manage a successful career while indulging in drugs and alcohol, while others cannot touch any of it without falling hard or fading away. Both Jimmy and Selina have gone through the misery of a heavy addiction before they switched to Talwin, but they now put in a full day's work and seem to get on okay with their lives. Unlike Jodie, Jimmy is a criminal with or without the drug use. Every addict I meet is different, dealing with his or her addiction in a way that fits who they are.

"Can I ask you a question?" Jodie asked with genuine curiosity, the first time I bought heroin from her.

"Sure," I said.

"Who told you that I got?"

"Charlie."

She was polite. She went and checked with Charlie and then came back to sell to me. Other than her addiction, which she keeps to herself, she is strong and independent and I like dealing with her.

Across the table, a guy named Serge sits in between the two girls who work for him. Serge isn't a hype. He's a young, clean-looking, and friendly weed dealer. He sells his marijuana in the bars of Gastown and Davie Street and looks after the girls. Both Indigenous, they are young, pretty, and they seem to have a close relationship with him. Not into heroin, these three marijuana dealers very seldom come to the Blackstone, but prefer the bars of Gastown where the weed business is better. If they come up Granville Street, they usually sit in the lounge of the Austin. They are quiet, except when they bring their heads close together to exchange a few words and a laugh. This afternoon, Serge came to the Blackstone to party with Jimmy. He isn't into heroin so I stay away from business talk with him.

Everyone is relaxed and this is building up to be a good night with the Blackstone putting on its party face. Some of the regular old-timers are even getting into it, hitting the dance floor with fancy ballroom moves, while up a few steps from the main floor, Scotty is now busy winning at the pool table, taking on anyone who places a quarter on the table's edge.

After a while, a man comes to our table and asks for H.

"You don't look like a user," I say.

"I just did it once. I want to try it again.... It's a good high."

"Fuck off," I say, looking away.

Jimmy looks on, ready to jump in. I'm just doing what everybody else does when a new face comes in the Blackstone looking to score heroin, but it also makes me feel good to turn away someone looking for drugs. If there is anything that makes undercover work worthwhile, it's the paranoia it creates with the traffickers, getting in the way of quick and easy deals. But it isn't much because, in the end, people like to get together to get high, whether it's alcohol, weed, cocaine, or heroin. It's universal. Since I've been here, I've made a few friends in the Blackstone and the better the friend, the more encouragement and advice I got on how to become a true addict. Not one of my friends told me to stay away from junk. My friends even showed me how to use, and if I told them that I puked on the floor after fixing, they were glad and we all laughed. When I was just starting, Kangaroo told me to add the citric acid, and when the heroin was good and strong, both Deedee and Jodie said to do a half so I wouldn't OD. There is nothing here to stop someone from using heroin for the first time. Nothing except for the cops and the paranoia they create. No one is prepared for that first hit of heroin, and I'm glad that tonight none of my friends will teach this guy how to mainline a cap of it.

"When are you going to Prince George?" Jimmy asks, all business.

"Tomorrow," I say, thinking that I have the weekend to myself and am looking forward to a camping trip to the Sunshine Coast, hundreds of miles away from Prince George.

"I saw my guy at the Austin earlier," he continues. "He has bundles. He's not cheap but his stuff is the best around. He's a good guy and he can help you out. We can go see if he's there."

I've waited a long time for this, but I don't want to look too eager.

"You sure he's got good stuff?"

"Yeah, the best. Everybody's buying from him."

Jimmy goes to Serge and says something to him. Serge nods to Melanie, one of the two girls sitting with him, and she pulls out an eight ball of weed from her purse and gives it to him. Jimmy winks at Serge.

"Let's go," he says looking at me.

We walk across to the Austin, but the guy isn't there, so we go up to Jimmy and Selina's apartment. We climb the creaking stairs to his small loft, on the second floor of a two-storey building. The apartment is clean. On the windowsill overlooking Davie Street, pink flowers cascade down from a brown ceramic pot onto the small kitchen table. We sit at the table and Jimmy rolls a joint.

"This is a good place," I say.

"Yeah, we can walk everywhere from here."

Jimmy lights up the joint.

"How long have you lived here?"

"Two years."

Jimmy and I are both from Québec. He already told me that he came from a small town in the Beauce region.

"You ever go back home?"

"No, never," he says handing me the joint. "Things are good here. Where I come from there's nothing, man. Just fucking nothing."

"I'm from Montréal, but I like the country," I say. "Me and my dad we used to go fishing up north. He'd find a lake in the middle of nowhere. We'd have it to ourselves. We'd follow a trail up a mountain for hours and find some fucking rowboat sitting there, waiting for us ...on top of a mountain! ...in the middle of nowhere! And there it was, a fucking leaking rowboat with an empty tobacco can in it so you can bail the water out. How it got there in the first place, man, I can't figure it out. We fished all day with nobody else on the lake."

Jimmy takes a long drag and holds it, his eyes watering.

"We did a lot of hunting where I lived," he says after letting out a trail of smoke. "My dad used to fish too. He was tough, man. You didn't fuck with him, his hands the size of frying pans. He'd give you a slap on the side of the head, make you feel dizzy. What does your dad do?"

"He drives big rigs, all across the country, but mainly in Québec."

"My dad's a mechanic. He fixes big rigs, tractor trailers."

"Oh yeah? Hey, maybe your dad fixed my dad's truck one time." Jimmy laughs. "Maybe they went fishing together."

We both laugh at that. We're almost done with the joint so Jimmy stands up and I follow him to the door at the top of the stairs.

"Fishing's good here, we should rent a boat sometime, and go salmon fishing," Jimmy says.

"Can Selina clean fish?"

"Yeah, fuck, she can. She knows how to use a knife."

"Okay, we catch the fish and Selina cooks it."

Jimmy and I look at each other and break into a laugh.

"Yeah, fuck, you and me on a fucking boat."

We sit side by side on the steps, at the top of the stairs, laughing. I pass him the joint for one last time.

"You have it made," I say. "Selina is a good-looking girl."

"Yeah, she's the best.... You should see her cunt." Jimmy brings his hands together as if holding something precious. "She has the most perfect cunt."

Jimmy turns serious and looks me in the eyes.

"We can make things happen you and me," he says.

He takes a last drag and I follow him down the stairs and out into the fresh, humid air.

"If you do it right, you can make some good money here with the right connection," he continues. "I know a lot of people."

"I have some good people in George right now," I say. "All I need is a good connection in Vancouver. People I can trust."

"That's the whole thing," Jimmy says. "You have to have the right people."

"They're waiting for me right now. They'll buy whatever I have, but I have to take my time."

"This guy can help you."

"Prince George is good and easy, but here, things are way too hot ...way too hot. I don't want to deal around here. And I don't want to deal with a guy who's got heat on him."

"I know," Jimmy says. "I'll get you hooked up with this guy. He has the best stuff around and the cops don't know him either. He never did time. It'll be good for you ...but don't forget me."

We walk into the Blackstone. Selina isn't back from the street yet so we cross to the Austin to see if Jimmy's contact is there.

The Austin isn't really a heroin bar and its staff takes a hard stance against the hookers and heroin users who may wander in. They kick them out when they are too obvious. It also brings in performers to attract a better class of clients. When we enter the bar, it has already filled up with patrons eager to see a stripper who, as they advertise, can both play the flute and shoot ping-pong balls out of her vagina.

Jimmy leaves me sitting alone at a table while he goes looking for his man. He comes back a few minutes later with a tall and fairly stocky, chubby-faced man wearing a track suit and runners. They stop near the lobby door where the man listens and Jimmy talks. After a while, the man throws a glance at me and then comes to the table.

"Max," he says, extending his hand.

"Nick ...Jimmy told me you could help me out."

Max listens to me as I speak about my business in Prince

George and how I can move heroin on a regular basis up there. Like most drug traffickers dealing with a new client, Max is a mix of cockiness and fear. He exudes confidence and control as he listens to me selling myself, but his eyes search the bar for anything that doesn't fit. To him, as with any drug dealer, the customer is the biggest asset, but he is also the biggest threat. He leans slightly forward on his chair.

"I can help you."

"Great, I'm looking for something steady. I want something regular, a good steady supply."

"When are you leaving?" he asks as a ping-pong ball comes bouncing near our table.

"Tomorrow morning," I say.

Max picks up the white ball and throws it back at the men near the stage who reach out for it like a group of bridesmaids trying to catch the bouquet.

"I can't do anything till about four o'clock tomorrow," he says, smiling at the crowd.

"Okay, I'll wait," I say, thinking that I would have to cancel my camping trip.

"Did Jimmy tell you the price? ...575," he says, still smiling.

"Yeah, it's a bit heavy."

"My smack is the best around. Not the shit you get across the street. Pure white ...the best around. You won't regret it. How many do you want?"

"Two."

"Yeah, okay. Good. Be here at four."

Max cocks his head to the side and smiles. "Listen," he says, "do you hear it?"

A few notes from a flute can now be heard among the laughter coming from the crowd.

TWO BUNDLES

The next day I drive down Davie and cross Granville Street to turn into the lane where I park my car. It's a warm and sunny day, and if everything goes right, this day will be the beginning of my new life as a bundle dealer. I feel the roll of money tucked inside my boot, and unlike most days when I begin my shift in the Blackstone, I take the alley and go directly to the Austin, eager to see if Max will come through.

Inside, the place is quiet, except for a few pool players. I'm surprised to see Charlie sitting alone at a table. Like most hypes, he almost never hangs out in the Austin where the beer costs more than the Blackstone. I walk up to him.

"Hey, what's going on?"

"You looking?"

"No, I've already got something going."

"He'll be in later."

I sit down beside him and order a couple of beers. Charlie knows that I am waiting for Max, so I assume that Max has gone to him to see if I am good to deal with. My time spent with him finally paid off. After a while, Jodie also comes in and sits with us.

The heroin I had bought from her was clean China white, almost ten per cent pure, and it differed a lot from the regular brown "number three" heroin or "apple juice" you normally find on the Strip. When she sold it to me, Jodie was very careful to warn me not to do too much. If an addict regularly does two caps at two per cent, he could easily die if the two caps contain ten per cent heroin, which would be like doing ten caps. The price is the same, thirty-five dollars a cap and nothing tells you to hold back and not do it all at once unless the dealer warns you. The cover team is aware of this new supply and we heard that some users overdosed on it. We expected the purity to come down once the dealers realized that they could easily quadruple their profit, but this isn't happening.

Jodie also asks about Max and I figure that both she and Charlie get their good product from him.

The waiter comes to the table.

"If you guys don't drink, you have to get out of here," he says looking us down. Jodie smiles at him and orders some beer.

"You guys do your shit outside," he says, before leaving to get the beer.

Hypes bring heat with them wherever they go. I need to distance myself so I leave the table without a word and walk to a spot near the strippers' empty stage. After a while, Max suddenly appears. He didn't come from outside, so I assume that he came from somewhere in the hotel. He looks at me and walks out. About twenty minutes later, he comes back, looks around, and disappears again. The agreed time has passed, but Max seems to be working to make this deal happen. I pull the money out of my boot and put it in my pocket. Unlike the hypes of the Blackstone, Max blends well with the Austin regulars and deals with the staff on equal, friendly terms. He casually walks out again. Delays are the norm in drug deals, especially with a new buyer, but I begin to feel like nothing is going to happen for a while, if at all. A few minutes later, Jimmy comes in to see me.

"You think he can do it?" I ask, anxious to score and leave.

"Don't worry, it's coming," he says, lowering his eyelids for effect.

When Max comes in again, I expect some heat, but he sits next to me and gets right into it.

"You got the money?" he asks.

"Yeah."

He moves his hand next to my thigh and drops the two bundles I ordered into mine—fifty caps I can still cut and sell for fifty dollars apiece in Prince George.

I pull the roll of money out of my pocket, $1,150 in total, and give it to him.

"You can count it if you want," I say.

"I trust you," he answers with a smile.

Max pockets the money and leaves. I turn to Jimmy.

"Thanks," I say.

He nods and closes his eyes again.

I am rich.

DEALERS AND JUNKIES

A few days later, I park my car behind Theo's and take a walk around the block. Selina and Maggie are standing on their corner, walking a few steps here and there and bending over to wave at some of the drivers who slow down to take a better look at them.

"How's it going?" I ask Selina.

"Good," she says with a smile. "Jimmy's inside."

Maggie gives me a wave and I keep on walking to the Blackstone while they get back to business.

I am pleased with my story. The heroin I bought from Max analyzed at just under ten per cent. This is high for the streets, especially in Prince George, and I can justify a story where the two bundles I bought for just over a thousand dollars were cut again to two or three per cent, and sold in Prince George for a return around $5,000.

"How did it go in Prince George?" Jimmy asks.

"Great," I reply. "I stepped on it because it was too good, but it was still the best over there. I worked all night emptying all the caps and adding the buffer, but it was worth it. At fifty bucks a cap it's worth it."

"You can make a lot of money up there if you're careful."

"I'm gonna give it some time before I go back. Let things cool down a little."

"Good ...good, take your time."

"Couldn't believe how much cut it took," I continue with enthusiasm. "It was still good for up there ...fucking crazy. I sold it all in a couple of days and then I gave a few bundles on the cuff. I'll get the rest of my money when I go back."

"I told you, you could trust him. If you want, I can go with you next time."

"Sure ...I'll let you know. Why don't you work with Max?" I ask, awkwardly.

"Don't worry about me," he says dryly. "I'm doing stuff with him, like I do with you. I don't deal around here. I don't want to go back to where I was before."

"Yeah, we're the same you and me. I'm gonna take it easy for a few days and then we can talk."

For the first time, I find myself above the action of the Blackstone and it affects how I deal with people. I'm also learning from Jimmy. He found his place on the street and it works for him and this is why we get along. There is also some legitimate respect between him and me. To him it's black and white, crime and money, and so it is for me. I can relate to that. He doesn't deal in the Blackstone, and he's not on our target list, but he's made up his mind about me and he knows a lot of the people the cover team is interested in.

In the following days, I no longer talk about caps. Instead, I speak of buying and selling bundles. I also clean up the way I look just enough to make people believe that my drug deals are yielding more than a needle in my arm.

Like Max, I spend more time in the Austin, and when it's time to talk business or wait for a deal to come through, I will sometimes walk a couple of blocks to the Yale, away from the heat. I don't sit anywhere for too long. The next day I enter the Blackstone and take a seat alone against the wall. Maggie comes in alone and walks over to my table.

"Are you looking?" she asks.

"No, I'm just taking it easy. I did a good score last week, got something going."

"My old man has some good action, if you're interested."

"Can he get bundles?"

"You'd have to talk with him. He'll make you a good price."

Jodie comes in and sits with us.

"How's it going?" I ask.

Jodie lets out a long sigh. "I need a vacation."

"What's the matter?"

"I lost my job so I guess I'm on vacation now, but like a change of scenery's what I need."

"You should go on a trip."

"If you give me some money I will. I could go to Bangkok and we could do business there. It's easy, you know, I've done it before. We could get a couple ounces of pure for nothing."

"I'll save my money," I say, "and maybe we can make it a real vacation."

From now on, the dealers know that I am no longer dependent on them for caps and they want a part of my action. I feel like I am dealing with different people, people who see more value in me than I see in them. Whenever Jodie, Captain Kangaroo, Charlie, or Chico come in and see me, they sit at my table and we talk about the action. Everything is about heroin, who's got and how good it is. People come in to score, sometimes just out of jail or in transit, and everyone has an angle.

I still play the user, always aiming for new targets, buying a cap whenever I can for my own fix. We talk about the good and the bad heroin going around and pass used needles—our "rigs"—to each other. In the Blackstone against the wall everything is about heroin, whether you sell it or use it.

Since the night she ripped me off at the beginning of the operation, I stayed away from Cindy. With her old man out of jail, she is now even busier doing rips, knowing that he is there to protect her. They seldom sell heroin and prefer to rip people off, with or without violence, and she seems to always have something going with one unlucky mark or another.

None of that interests me on the business side, but I like to watch them in action, Cindy and her old man. They are like sharks cruising the waters, waiting to come across something they can feed on. They aren't dangerous to me because I know to stay away. Undercover work is like that. It gives you an advantage. Not like doing a routine stop in uniform, where the people in the car you stop know who you are before you have a chance to find out anything about them. I know Cindy and her old man well, and I know how bad they hate the police, so I would rather be undercover with them in the Blackstone, than stop them randomly on a roadside checkstop.

Knowing who you are dealing with is the trickiest thing when you come in cold into a bar. It takes time to know who to stay away from. I now watch the new faces walk in, with their fish-out-of-water expression, just to get hooked up with Cindy. They are looking for drugs or girls or anything else that can be obtained on the street. Seeing a mark sitting alone at a table and waiting while Cindy runs around reminds me of my first days in the Blackstone. Only when I see Cindy walk out with the mark do I regret not to be able to get involved in some way. Spanky usually follows and I know that the mark might get hurt. Whatever it's about, it's ugly any way you look at it. On one night, I saw Cindy beat up a hooker on the sidewalk of Granville Street. The girl was down and Cindy was sinking her high heels deep into her belly. Spanky stood across the street, watching.

And yet, they make a nice-looking couple, the tall, clean-cut, dark and handsome man, and the small brunette with the pretty blue eyes. The kind of people you would want to rent your house to, if appearance was all you had.

An Asian girl I know as Angie comes and sits next to me. She doesn't say a word, just sits there. I am tired and don't really want to deal with anyone new, so I drink my beer and chat with Scotty who comes over between games of pool for a sip of his beer. A few people come and go, but Angie stays at my side. A while later, Kitty comes and sits with us. She has a problem with someone who owes her money.

"When you give your word you have to honour it!" she vents, like a disgruntled mother.

I agree with her and she seems satisfied.

More people come and go and Angie remains silent, next to me. I buy her a beer and it makes me feel strong to have her sit next to me. For a man sitting in this bar, it makes a difference to have a woman at your side, especially if you pay no mind to her. Jimmy and Harry do it well, and like them, I sit next to her and look ahead at the crowd of people going about their business. At the end of the night, she tells me that she has to go.

"I work on Main Street ...have my own corner."

"That's good," I say still looking ahead.

Above us the speakers are blasting "Back on the Chain Gang" and I like the song.

"You want to be my old man?" she asks.

The voice is faint and I am not sure I heard her right.

"I need somebody to look after me.... You want to be my old man?"

I turn to her. She looks tired. Nothing in her suggests that she looks forward to standing on that street corner. The lower part of Main is rough, even for hookers, and I don't want to think about the wicked and desperate johns she meets there on a daily basis.

"No ...sorry."

"I'll look after you."

She is looking at me straight, waiting for an answer.

"I already have an old lady," I say.

Angie gets up and I watch her quietly walk out of the bar.

Like other police officers, when I began this operation I looked at the Blackstone as a box of crime and violence. It was the easiest way to look at it. Now, everyone has a story and it's becoming increasingly difficult to be detached from it. The heroin scene is like a fast freeway where everyone rushes past. Some have just begun their journey and some are well into it, cruising along. Some, like Angie, may not make the next curve.

I look at Scotty hustling deals by the pool table, laughing. He'll be on the nod soon. Meanwhile, Deedee walks in and meets a group of friends sitting near the front door. Like Scotty, heroin is a part of her lifestyle. I can have a normal conversation with her and I don't mind her company, but I can't think of anywhere else where she would be accepted as she is. Like many of the other addicts around me, the Blackstone is her village.

And no one has more power in this village than the bundle dealers. Local bundle dealers never come down to the Blackstone unless they are looking for someone, usually to collect. They are in for the business first, even if many of them are also users. They have the heroin connection and make a living out of it. Everything above them is business and everything below is about using. If heroin were legal, our work wouldn't be that different because these people are criminals first and they would be selling better heroin at the black market price. And more easy access to heroin means more junkies, anyway you look at it. Bundle dealers are easy to spot in the Blackstone because they usually walk in looking for someone, their hands in their pockets and a determined look on their faces. I know a few of them from their pictures and criminal history. There are the two Albanian brothers, balding men in their forties, who always walk fast through the bar. If they see the person they are looking for, they go to them and say a couple words before leaving. They are violent men and the story is that, a while back, they were dishing out a vicious beating to a man when the police arrived. They ran away only to show up later at the hospital to finish the job. Many of the Eastern European traffickers have good connections with importers from the old country. Dealing every day with street junkies and informants is complicated and the dealers must use violence to make a go of it. The business demands a ruthless disposition and fear is the cement that holds everything together.

When a known bundle trafficker walks in, I recognize him right away from my days as a uniformed officer in White Rock. He was a young kid then, one who broke into houses and sold weed. Any day of the week, if you looked for him you could find him standing in front of the local pool hall and staring at cars driving by. I remember him well because at fourteen, he had already been involved in a gun incident. No one was hurt, but we needed to take caution when dealing with him in our small, sleepy town.

I already knew that meeting him in the Blackstone was a possibility because I saw his picture at the Shack. This was a serious concern for the cover team not only because he could easily burn my cover, but also because he is a violent man who, only a year ago, had lured an undercover operator to an isolated area where the officer was beaten up and robbed.

He walks directly to our table and pulls a seat. I turn and chat with Captain Kangaroo, sitting at the table next to me. The bundle dealer looks around him, searching. He says something to Kitty and she shakes her head. When we finally make eye contact he doesn't recognize me. To him, I am a faceless junkie on the Granville Strip. He is the Man and he is looking for somebody and that somebody isn't me. He's not here to deal, but to settle a score, so we drink beer and I ignore him while he does his business with the other dealers.

There is a lot of violence dished out by the bundle dealers to the street users, but things are often handled more delicately when it's time to kill. Killing a street addict is probably the easiest thing in the world for his supplier. It only takes a special treat of fifty per cent heroin to make sure that the junkie's life will end in a sad, quiet death. A dead body would be found in a grungy hotel room and the cops would learn from an informant that the user was hot capped. That information would be put on a debriefing report only to be read by other cops because, on its own, it is useless in court. At the end, a junkie would stop showing up, and unless someone talks and is ready to testify, the case will be closed.

I see the two sides of the junkies' story. In the bar, I see them live their addiction in the best way they can, making friends and sticking together, sometimes sick and sometimes on the nod. And whenever I get back to my desk and its police reports, I see a stream of drug arrests, punctuated by other crimes such as assaults or some forms of theft or robbery. On occasion, one of them will stop coming to the bar and, a few days later, on his or her picture along the wall will appear the letters DOA, written by hand across the face in a greasy pen.

MARKS

We never watch the strippers in the Austin, but this one is different. Jimmy, Max, and I have taken a table near the stage where we watch the giant blond woman she claims to weigh 450 pounds—doing a stand-up comedy act that has everyone laughing out loud. A group of sailors are in town and blowing off steam at a large table. One of them, a small man with a big haggling voice, volunteers to go on the stage. The stripper puts a blindfold on him and sits him on a chair in the middle of the floor. She then circles him like a great white shark, the crowd silenced by a feeling that something ominous is going to happen. I don't know if this is a set-up, but she pounces on him and, in one swift move, stuffs his head into the front of her panties and pulls him up by the back of his pants, carrying him upside down in a victory circle, the shine of his boots catching the lights as she walks around in a sea of applause and laughter.

Once the show is over, the regular strippers take their turn and we head back to the lounge.

Given the quality of Max's heroin, there is a good chance that he gets his supply in powder form and then does the cutting and capping himself.

"Listen," I tell Max, "I want to go back up north, but scoring bundles is way too much work, with emptying the caps and all."

"I have a connection for good powder," he says with a glint in his eyes. "Let's talk later."

Serge comes down with the two girls so we stop talking heroin. Strictly a weed dealer, Serge is a quiet guy, almost shy, and he is always in the company of the girls. He listens and shakes his head as we tell him about the giant stripper. The girls giggle.

Serge tells me that he has a pound of skunk weed and wants to know if I am interested.

"You have some left?" he asked Melanie who sits at his side.

Melanie opens her purse and pulls out a small baggie. She pinches a small bulb and brings it to my nose. Her hand is delicate and her nails are clean and shiny. The weed is pungent. She puts the weed back in the bag and wipes her hand on a napkin.

"Sticky," she says.

"Looks good," I say, "but I'm not into it."

"Weed's the way to go, man," Serge says. "There's too much heat on junk and you won't get time if you get caught with weed."

Serge looks like your average weed dealer from high school. He is sociable and seems to make friends easily. He likes cars and drives a Mustang.

"Classic green," he says, "original stripes."

"I love that car," I say. "I have a beater, but it gets me where I want to go."

A man comes and sits next to Serge. He could be coming straight out of a disco with his designer jeans and a clean shirt with the collar open over his short leather jacket. He has a thin moustache and his hair is done in a mullet. Everything about him, including the timid look on his face, says that he belongs somewhere else. Serge turns to Jimmy and me and says the guy has some coke.

"Come here," Jimmy says with a frown. "What have you got?"

Jimmy takes on his serious street look. The man walks up to him.

"I have some good blow," he says with a weak smile. "I usually don't deal but I need the money."

"Show me."

The man sits next to Jimmy and carefully unfolds a square of score paper cut out from a magazine.

"I can let you have the whole gram for one-fifty."

A small mound of loosely packed snow sparkles on the shiny creased paper. Jimmy moves the paper so it sits directly in front of him.

"I could get two-fifty for this," the man continues.

The man leans forward, but his chair is too far away from the table so he rests his elbows on his thighs, which make him look nervous and affable, more like a mark than a coke dealer. His leg jumps like the needle of a sewing machine. Jimmy feeds on this nervousness.

"I want to try it first," he says, looking closely at the powder.

Without a word, the man moves closer and lays a line of the cocaine in front of Jimmy, chopping at it with a credit card until he has a neat, short line.

Serge doesn't need that kind of heat so he gets up with the girls.

"Talk to you later," he says to Jimmy, throwing a glance at the man. The girls smile and the three of them leave.

Jimmy rolls a bill and inhales the powder up his nose.

"It's not very good," he says. "Try it, Nick."

"No thanks," I say, looking around the empty lounge.

"It's good Peruvian flake," says the man, "ninety per cent."

"Let me try it again."

I never get how it is that we need to settle into roles like this. I guess it's easier to go along and find your place in a group than it is to go against the grain. It's as if somewhere along the line, the man and Jimmy agree that the former is the mark. That he is ready to be fucked over. It's not about the bad coke. Dealers like Crowley and Cindy also sell bad drugs once in a while. It's this guy who brings it on by being weak and remaining there, even after the abuse has started. He made a mark of himself and can't stop it. Can't get away.

"Give me another one!" repeats Jimmy.

The man carefully lays another line down and Jimmy sniffs it in.

"That stuff is shit! I wouldn't pay a fucking dime for it. Put another one down!"

The man is hesitant.

"Put another one down."

The man lays another line.

"Try it, Nick. That stuff is shit."

I laugh. Jimmy will use up all he could from the guy's supply, good or not.

"No thanks, I'm good."

Jimmy inhales half the line of white powder.

"You try to sell that shit here you gonna get killed," he says angrily.

He sniffs the other half.

"That stuff is fucking shit! Get the fuck out of here. You're gonna get killed. You try to sell this shit here somebody's gonna kill you."

The man has a dumb friendly smile on as if he doesn't understand.

"Get the fuck out of here!"

The next day I learn from the cover team that a man was killed in the Blackstone at around the same time. One of the regulars had lured him into the washroom where he slit his throat. He was just another mark, like the guy with the coke, an outsider too clean-looking for the place and too young to know better.

The cover team wants me to see if people are talking about the homicide, so I go to the Blackstone and meet Captain Kangaroo sitting alone smoking a cigarette.

"I heard someone got shivved last night," I say.

"I saw him ...came out of the washroom. It was like somebody poured a whole bucket of blood on the front of his shirt."

INTERLUDE
(PART I)

When I see Harry walk into the Blackstone a few feet ahead of his girl, staring at me and swaying his broad shoulders through the bar until he reaches my table, I know that he has action.

"Do you have it?" he asks.

"Yeah," I say, feeling the lump of rolled up money pressing against my ankle.

I follow him out. Maggie walks quietly behind me. She arranged the deal and worked out the price with me, but Harry is the boss and he has the connection.

"Where's your car?" he asks.

"Behind Theo's."

We walk across the street to my car in the back parking lot and Harry directs me to drive on to Helmcken Street. After we make the first turn, he twists his body and scans the streets behind us searching for heat. We drive down Hastings, which takes us out of the downtown core and past the PNE with its large wooden roller coaster. Harry keeps his head on a swivel, looking left, looking right, his eyes locking on cars going by, trying to see if we are being followed. It's rush hour and vehicles of all sorts are around us, passing us, their occupants staring ahead without expression, lone men and women leaving downtown after work tired and lost in their thoughts. Harry looks at them all, trying to find anything that doesn't fit. All concentration. All action.

"Turn here!"

Just past the PNE, Harry has me park in an empty lot. He walks to a pay phone and picks up the receiver. I see two unmarked police cars go by, a bit faster than the rest of the cars driving by and with more purpose. Both cars go to the next corner where they turn off in different directions. I am hoping that Harry didn't see them, but it's too late. Harry is already looking for the heat and his attention is fixated on them. He hangs up the telephone and jumps back into my car.

"We gotta go!"

We drive off and pass one of the cars, sitting in a dark parking lot. Harry stares at it. Two guys are in it.

"Fuck!"

We go slowly around the block and Harry keeps looking back. I can see Maggie's wide open eyes in my rear-view mirror, nervously scanning around her. When we approach Boundary Road, I drop them off on the side of the road. They will not be getting their fix tonight.

I drive away without looking back, wondering if they are blaming the heat on me.

INTERLUDE
(PART II)

The next day I walk into the Blackstone early to see if the heat we took the night before has spilled onto me. It was my car that the cops followed, and I know that Harry and Maggie likely spent the night talking about me, about the heat, and about the different scenarios that could have led the cops to us. From Harry's perspective, the heat is either on me or on him. I want to get a feel for what he thinks, and get in on any discussions and accusations before any damage is done.

As I walk in, I see Captain Kangaroo and the Accountant talking animatedly. I already know from my experience with Frank that heat can spread in the Blackstone like wildfire, and I keep my head up as I approach the table. But all I get is an indifferent glance from Kangaroo as he listens to the Accountant talking about a girl who sold him bad heroin. The Accountant looks at me to make his point while I take a seat next to him.

"I fixed it and there was nothing. There was less than nothing.... She ripped me!"

"Who's that?" I ask.

Before the Accountant can answer, Harry arrives at the table with Maggie. Like the previous day, he stares straight at me.

"Harry knows her!" the Accountant says looking at Harry. "The girl who used to come with her old man ...the tall skinny guy with the peak cap. You know who it is, Harry. What was her name? I can't remember...."

"I don't know who you're talking about."

Harry just stands there in front of me; he's not interested in some girl selling bad heroin. He ignores Kangaroo and stares at me, with Maggie standing a few feet behind. He sniffles and a quick shiver runs through his body. I am prepared to get some heat, but instead, he swallows hard.

"You want to go?" he asks.

"Yeah ...sure."

I get up and follow him out, leaving the Accountant to finish his gripe alone with Kangaroo.

Harry walks straight to the door and this time, there's no sway in him. Maggie walks behind us as we make our way to my car, just like we did the day before.

"Same place?" I ask.

"Yeah."

We drive east on Hastings again, but Harry isn't looking for heat anymore. Instead, he keeps his head straight and looks ahead of him like a horse with blinders on. He swallows hard again and sighs a few times. Harry doesn't want to see the heat, he's sick and wants his fix.

We pass the Sun building again where, only a year back, Clifford Olson, the killer of children, stood in the well-padded lawyer's office. I was a junior investigator then, keeping him company while tired senior investigators and his lawyers worked on the deal that would eventually lead us to his victim's bodies, making sure that he would remain in jail for the rest of his life. Now, barely a year later, sitting in a car with two heroin addicts going to score a couple of bundles, I realize how different the drug game is. I am a policeman, but this isn't about killing or robbing. It's about the drug. We are together in this car because the game is all about the drug, and we are playing it because on that sunny afternoon, a couple of drug addicts need to score their fix.

"Are you sure he'll be home?" asks Maggie from the back seat.

Harry sighs. "Why the fuck are you asking again? I already told you."

We stop at the same pay phone, but this time Harry walks up to it without looking around. The heat could be on him from all sides, but he doesn't care. He makes the call.

"What did he say?" Maggie asked as soon as he returns.

"He's waiting."

"Does he have it?"

"What the fuck do you think?"

We go almost as far as Boundary Road, a long way from the Granville Strip and its hypes and drug cops, and turn onto a small residential street where Harry points to a spot alongside a small city park. I park my car along the curb and look all around me. The two hypes are sick and I have to watch out for a rip, but I can't see anything that doesn't fit.

We are well into spring and the afternoon is quiet and mild. In the park, a couple of kids play on a slide under the watchful eyes of their mother.

Harry asks for the money and I give it to him without reserve. Something in his look, a strange mix of despair and resolve, along with the fact that his girl is sitting in the back of my car, tells me that he is coming back with the stuff.

Maggie and I wait silently. One of the kids stands at the top of the slide.

"Watch me," he yells at his mom.

We all watch.

"We're not supposed to be here," Maggie says after a while.

When Harry comes back, he walks quick and tight, hunched over with his hands in his pockets. He climbs into the car.

"I have to get water," he says, picking up an empty Coke bottle, lost in the food wrappers and other junk lying on the floor of my car.

I drive off and Harry holds a closed hand to my side, his thick fingers curled in around something. I put my hand out and he drops two bundles into it, a blue and a red balloon almost golf ball size and full of heroin caps. Holding the two bundles makes me feel good and I put them in my jacket pocket. Harry holds two more bundles. He unties the knot to one of the bundles and gently pulls six caps out of it. In a deft move, he ties the knot back and pulls the opening end of the balloon back over itself so that the package forms a perfectly round ball. He stuffs the two bundles back into his coat pocket. We stop at a gas station and Harry goes to the outside washroom, but the door is locked.

"Fuck!" Maggie groans.

Harry goes around the building to get the key then goes back to the washroom. A few minutes later he comes back to the car with the water.

"Let's go," he says.

"What are you doing?" Maggie asks impatiently.

"What do you think I'm doing?" he says before telling me to pull over again.

Harry pulls out an old aspirin tin and he pours some of the water into it.

"Hurry up!" Maggie cries.

"Shut the fuck up."

"What are you doing?" she asks again, exasperated.

"Shut the fuck up!"

"Don't be an asshole," she moans.

Harry empties three heroin caps in the water. The powder is brown and the resulting mixture looks like filthy dishwater. The looks of it would have given me pause, but Harry immediately pulls out a Bic lighter and cooks it until bubbles form. He then sucks the juice into the syringe through a torn up, used cigarette filter and looks for a vein on the inside of his wrist. The needle slides under the skin and a flag of red blood entering the syringe tells him that he has found it. Harry pushes the plunger in and the brownish juice disappears from the syringe. Harry then cooks a second mixture and pulls it into his syringe. I drive off again.

"I don't want to stay here too long," I say.

Harry turns around over the seat and I watch him through the rear-view mirror trying to inject the dark juice into Maggie's neck. The needle is well through the skin, but he can't find the vein. Maggie's face twists from pain as the needle explores the inside of her neck, changing direction within the muscle and going in deep and then back.

"Don't fuckin' move!" Harry tells her.

Harry prods deeper into her neck. Maggie clinches her teeth.

"Fuck!" she yells.

"Stop the car!" Harry orders.

I stop on a quiet street again. A man waters his front lawn a couple of houses away, his silhouette darkening under a reddening sun. The dry afternoon air is settling into the cool stillness of the evening. Harry gets out with Maggie. She leans back against the hood of the car and he leans over her. She is now lying flat on the hood and he is on top of her, his legs stretching back to keep contact on the ground. He holds the syringe to her neck and strains to steady it. The man looks on and traffic goes by, but even if Harry is no longer sick, he doesn't give a fuck about the heat, or the two bundles stuffed in his jacket pocket, which will get him some decent jail time if he is caught.

Maggie has her arms braced around his back to steady him. He is now draped over her, placing the needle carefully. To the man watering his lawn, they probably look like lovers playing around.

From inside my car, I watch the lovers, desperate partners in pain. Then it happens and they both relax, Maggie still lying on the hood of my car, and Harry on top of her, spent. Once they are back into my car, I drive off and pass the man watering his lawn. He doesn't look up.

"I can't take you back downtown ...not with what I'm holding," I say. "I have to go up north."

Harry and Maggie don't seem to care. I pull over and drop them off on a street corner, alone and silent. They both look on and wave as I drive off into the traffic.

CAPPING UP

It's Tuesday afternoon in the Austin Hotel and finding Max is easy. All I have to do is take a seat, order a beer, and wait for him to show up. Max's fiancée works at the Austin and he has made the hotel his place of business.

Max is my principal target now. Somehow he got his hands on some quality heroin and puts it out at three to five times the normal purity. It's either a mistake or a way to build his business, but it works and his stuff has been all over the streets. The problem is that it also landed him on our doorstep; Max wasn't on the target list when the operation began, but his picture is now on the wall back at the Shack.

Heroin comes and goes on the Granville Strip according to a variety of supply sources. The brownish number three heroin brought in from Asia or Mexico trickles in on a continual basis, showing up at two to three per cent on the street. It's the staple of street heroin users. Sometimes a shipment of glistening fresh kilos of pure white number four heroin will arrive in hollowed out coffee table legs stacked inside a marine container. Smaller quantities are also brought in by sailors in filthy cargo ships and by air travellers who swallow the drug or carry it in their rectums. This mix of different sources of supplies ensures that heroin is always available in some form or another.

I am just getting into my beer when I spot Max's smug face above the crowd. He scans the bar and his face lights up when he sees me.

"Haven't seen you in a while," he says, pulling up a chair.

"I was away for a few days ...just got back."

"Why didn't you come down and see me before you left?"

"I had something going ...just a one-time thing."

"Don't do one-time things, Nick. You'll get burned. Listen, I need a partner, someone to go with for a quarter ounce. It's all lined up. The best, same as before, you won't find anything else like it here. Then we cap it up and split the bundles."

Capping up means emptying out hundreds of tiny, pink and white, five-milligram Benadryl capsules so that they can be re-stuffed with street grade heroin. Since ounces of bulk heroin usually come out at around forty to seventy per cent, we would need to add milk sugar to it to bring it down to anywhere around two to five per cent. I need to be careful with the idea of a partnership, but buying powder with Max would likely get me to higher-level targets.

"Let's talk about it tonight," I say. "What am I looking at?"

"About two grand."

"I need to collect. You gonna be around tonight?"

"Yeah, I'll be around."

Later on in the evening Max is sitting with Victor, a dealer I've previously met, but with whom I've never done business before. I go directly to their table and take a seat.

"Hi Vic, how is it going?" I ask.

"It's Victor, man. If I wanted to be called Vic I would call myself that."

Max laughs at that. "Can you wait around a bit, I've got somebody I want you to meet."

I'm glad to see that Victor isn't Max's connection. He doesn't trust me, but he is close to Max and we sometimes sit at the same table and tolerate each other. Victor wears nice, expensive clothes that usually include a bright scarf. He carries an umbrella when it rains outside. He even carries an umbrella when it doesn't rain. He has done lots of time and keeps his business to himself. He's like one of those guys you see at a party, well dressed and articulate, sometimes with a nice car to drive, but who confounds people because nobody knows what he really does.

Except that I know that Victor gets his girlfriend to deal drugs for him. She takes all the risks, picking up the bundles from Max, or anyone else who happen to have them, and sells the caps on the street. Victor doesn't even need to touch the heroin. Victor's girlfriend is clean, lively, and hasn't been a user for long. She has no record and, given Victor's long history of drug trafficking, it's easy to imagine how it all started for her. Victor is careful with me and I never see him do or arrange a deal with anyone else. Some people gain importance by putting down others, and he is one of them, giving me heat whenever I am not around. Still, we hang around together with Max and his supply like a hyena and a vulture on a carcass, tolerating each other as long as there is enough for everyone.

I take Max aside to another table.

"Listen, if we're going to do business together, I want it to be just between you and me."

"Yeah, yeah."

"I mean ...I normally do things on my own. You and me, we need to look at it the same way."

"Yeah, nobody else is in this. You put in the two grand and it's only you and me."

"How much are you paying for the quarter?"

"Four thousand."

Max leans back in his chair. He twirls the keys in his hands and looks out at the bar crowd.

"That means I'm putting in half of it," I continue, looking at him.

Max stops twirling his keys and looks at me. "It's my connection, man."

I don't like it, but I want this deal to go ahead so I let it go.

"Okay, it's your connection, so I'll put in the two grand, but I want six out of it," I concede, knowing that it's still a good deal for him.

Max doesn't have to think about it for too long. If anything, I shortchanged myself and he will likely come out with at least twice as much. But I'm getting it for less than four hundred a bundle so the price is still good and I will nearly triple my investment. This is not the kind of deal I want, but he has the contact and in this game, the supplier is everything. Without a supplier, I'd be middling ready-made bundles or selling caps on the street and barely get my own fix out of it.

Even with a good connection, most user-dealers will never get off the street, injecting any profit into their arm. The more heroin they handle, the more they use until all profit disappears and they find themselves hustling deals of one or two caps for a two dollar commission. Their habit rules their lives and they never get out. With his connection—and being a non-user—Max can sit there with a smile on his face like a land baron controlling all the water.

Later in the evening a man wearing a bright red hockey team jacket comes looking for us. He smiles when his eyes connect with Max, and walks over. He's in his early twenties and has the boyish looks of a teenager. I wouldn't be surprised if he came straight from the hockey rink.

"Hey Joe, this is my partner, Nick."

Joe smiles. "It's ready. I just have to go and get it."

"I'm not fronting my money," I say.

"Okay, I'll ask if we can all go over there," he says amicably.

Cutting powder into the tiny street-level caps means a lot of work, so the idea is for Max to get a few of the trusted street dealers together and spend most of the night stuffing the caps. The cover team doesn't like it because it means going to a house and staying inside for hours with a pack of drug fiends we still don't know. There is also a code of conduct for capping up: no phone calls and no movement in or out of the house. This is a vulnerable time for heroin traffickers and is something most undercover officers don't get to do.

"We're doing it at your house, right?" Max says to Joe.

"Yeah, no problem."

Before we all split, Joe gives Max direction to his house in the East End, away from the heat of the Granville Strip.

I can't tell if Joe is a user. With his hair parted in the middle and carefully combed over his ears and his open collar shirt, he looks as if he is still in high school trying to be one of the cool kids. And he smiles a lot. He has an honest face and you could see a drug dealer trusting him. He doesn't talk money, so I know that, like Chico, he's a runner and has the trust of the supplier. We agree to meet at his house at nine o'clock.

To kill time, I cross Davie Street and go to the Blackstone. When I enter, two hookers are arguing loudly at a table and people move back when they stand up. One of the women throws a punch and by the time I reach Captain Kangaroo's table, the two hookers have turned into a tangled ball of fury.

Captain Kangaroo seems happy to see me. I take a seat next to him.

"Anything happening?" I ask, looking on as the waiters rush in and break up the fight.

"Nothing for now, Nick," he says in a friendly way.

He watches the people get back into their seats and lights up a cigarette. I wonder about his life. Like many of the other addicts in the Blackstone, he came from a life of crime, but it is difficult to say whether crime came as a result of drug addiction or the other way around. All I know is that Captain Kangaroo left a whole lot of baggage behind and is now resigned to feed his habit while maintaining some level of self-worth.

Chico is sitting a few tables away with a couple of rounders I haven't seen before. To him, crime and drugs are a business—a business he constantly fails at—and it's difficult to untangle drug use from it. Chico likes the scene and I can see him in a few years, sitting where Kangaroo now sits ...if he lives that long.

"What's Chico up to?" I ask.

"He brings the heat onto himself. That's what he does."

Kangaroo turns to me. "I'd stay away from him if I were you. These guys he's with are bad news."

Cindy comes in with her old man and sits with Chico. She can smell the violence in his friends and they like what they see in her. Spanky sits next to her, scanning the bar around him while she does all the talking. He rounds his back and keeps his head slightly down so that his eyes have to look up, more like an eel than a shark. He lost a lot of weight since the first day I saw him when he just came out of jail. His cheeks are sunken in and his eyes, empty. He is a heavy user and he has already lost the muscle weight and healthy build that intimidated everyone when he was released from jail, hungry for action. Heroin and the street are hurting him more than his time inside the joint.

Two guys from the Street Crew come in. One of them is small and clean-shaven, his hair combed back straight and neat. The other is a large man with a scruffy beard and thick curly hair. They walk slowly and chat together. As they get past Spanky, the smaller cop turns violently and jumps on him, his right hand on his throat. The other follows and the three disappear onto the floor. I then realize that a half dozen other cops have now come in and are looking over the scene.

Soon, Spanky is pulled up, his hands handcuffed behind his back. Today, it's his turn. They take him out the back door to the alley and everything returns to normal.

Kangaroo takes a drag off his cigarette.

When Max walks in it's easy for me to see that he has action. He walks briskly to my table.

"Do you have it?" he asks, his eyes scurrying the bar.

"Not with me ...give me fifteen. I'll get my car and come and pick you up."

I feel good about the deal, but I don't want Max to know that I have the money with me until we're on our way.

When I return to Davie and Granville, Max is standing with Charlie and his girlfriend Amy. Everything looks good. We make our way down Twelfth avenue and I look at Charlie's face in my rear-view mirror. Like the others, he seems relaxed. The car is quiet, no stupid and nervous jokes or private chats. We drive to a grey stucco house in Vancouver's East End near Renfrew Street. Joe meets us at the door with a woman at his side.

"This is my wife Rhonda," he says.

Rhonda is a short, chubby woman about twice his age with a friendly red face. A young teenager hangs around the kitchen.

I am tempted to object to the number of people in the room, but I don't want to raise the anxiety level. Joe calls his man and tells us that everything is ready for him to go and get the merchandise, but that I have to stay behind. Max sees that I am about to object.

"Give it to me. I'll be there the whole way. Nothing to worry about."

I turn to Joe. "That's not what you said."

"I talked to him and he didn't budge ...says that if he sees any-body else he'll cancel the deal."

Max and Joe both look at me.

"You can trust me with it," Max says.

"You're in my house, man. I gotta come back," says Joe.

I give the two grand to Max and he leaves with Joe to pick up the stuff. Once they are gone, I asked Charlie what he is making out of the deal.

"I don't know," he says shrugging his shoulders. "I'm not greedy."

All Charlie wants is for Max to put him into action so that he can sit in the Blackstone with a bundle in his mouth and have enough heroin left over to keep his young girlfriend happy. Amy looks vulnerable, standing next to him, her hands gripping the sleeves of her sweater the way a child does, but I know that she is a heavy user. She is also the expert in the room, and by Charlie's account, good at capping up and that's why he brought her. He is older than her by about twenty years, but they have a close relationship, the kind you develop by fixing together. Like all junkies, they can't unravel heroin from the other parts of their lives.

While we wait for Max, Rhonda takes us to the bedroom where she grabs a large expensive suitcase and opens it on the bed.

"We go to the airport once in a while. I picked up this one from the carousel last week. Take a look and see if you like anything. It's all for sale."

We rummage through golf shirts, dresses, and pants, some wrapped in dry-cleaning cellophane. Amy buys a pretty blouse.

"It can't be easy to take luggage from a carousel," I say, "with all the people watching."

"You have to look like you know the bag is yours," she says, "like, if you're stopped, you apologize. People just want to get out of there."

It looks to me like a lot of work for little profit, but Joe's wife seems to enjoy rummaging through the folded clothes, trying to find something anyone of us would like. The thing is, they are nice people, Joe and his wife, and I really mean it. I just don't think that they ever take a stance on anything. They offer their house for us to package heroin and they take bags from airport carousels because there is nothing stopping them from doing it. They have a teenager walking around the house and he seems happy. Their place is clean and one could say that they have a good home if it wasn't for the heroin and stolen clothes.

After a half hour, Max and young Joe are back, and Joe pulls a rolled-up plastic bag from inside the front of his pants. Max opens it and sticks his fingertip in the powder before dabbing it on his tongue.

"It's good stuff," he says looking at us with a smile.

I don't know how he can tell from the taste. Maybe it's the lack of sugar grit or the texture. I gather that he probably saw it done on TV, like Kojak used to do, and wants to show he knows his business.

Amy takes the bag of heroin and walks to the small kitchen table. Butting up against the wall, the table can only accommodate three people.

"I'm feeling it," Max says. "It's real good stuff."

The teenager is looking on with interest. Joe tells him to go upstairs and he walks off without a word. Amy goes to the kitchen cupboards. With Rhonda's help, she pulls out a measuring cup, a large plate, and a couple of sieves. She puts the equipment on the table and takes a seat. Joe puts a box of lactose on the table.

"Where are the caps?" Amy asks.

Max pulls a plastic bag from his jacket pocket and gives it to her. Amy looks inside the bag.

"It won't be enough," she says.

There is silence.

"That's bad. Nobody should leave the house," Amy says.

"What are we gonna do?" asks Charlie.

Max pulls a few bills from his wallet.

"Get some Benadryl," he says to Joe, "be careful ...and don't forget the balloons."

"I don't like this," Amy says. "That's not the way it's done."

Given that we don't have much choice, Joe puts on his hockey jacket and leaves again. I can see why he is good at running dope. He doesn't argue and does what needs to be done. He also doesn't look like a hype, which is going to help since he's going to clean the shelves of Benadryl in every drugstore in the area.

Amy sits her small frame at the end of the table and begins mixing the lactose with the heroin. The young girl with the blue eyes frowns as she passes the powder through the sieve. She mixes and then mixes it again, and then passes the mixture through the sieve, and then mixes again. These steps are critical because any variation in the strength anywhere in the mix could result in a cap full of heroin strong enough to kill someone or, "even worse," as Amy points out, "a cap with no heroin in it."

After working on it for a while, Amy pulls a spoon from the utensils drawer and bends it so it can sit nice and straight on the table.

"I won't put too much in for the first test," she says.

Amy places a tiny amount of the mixed powder in the spoon and adds water and a broken cigarette filter. She holds the flame of a Bic lighter under the mixture and, as soon as it bubbles, sucks the clear juice into a syringe. She flags a tiny red cloud of her blood into the syringe and pushes the whole thing in.

It doesn't take long for Max to break into a laugh.

"Look at her eyes!"

Amy's pupils have disappeared into tiny dots. Despite her young, fresh face, Amy is the hardest addict in the room, and I have no doubt that what she injected into her body would have killed me.

"I told you that stuff's good!" Max adds, his eyes wide open like a proud magician at the end of a trick.

And I see the reason why I do this job. As sad as it is to see Amy's head hang over the mound of powder, it's the sparkling smile Max gives me that keeps me going. The smile of money. Amy's head starts to droop down slowly over the table until her nose almost touch the loose powder piled up on the plate. Amy doesn't know anything about this stuff, but she didn't think twice about injecting it. She brings her head up, allowing us to contemplate her dead blue eyes.

Max laughs again. "That's stuff's too good," he says. "Look at her ...we have to cut it again."

Charlie takes over the sifters and adds more lactose. After some good work mixing and sifting, he places a small amount back in the spoon and adds water.

"Who wants to test it?" he asks.

"I'll try it," Rhonda says.

Rhonda takes the spoon and syringe to the washroom. When she comes back, we can tell that the stuff is still too good. She agrees.

"Let's add more cut," says Max, seeing his profit increase every time the lactose is added.

After more cut is sifted through, it's Charlie's turn to give it a try.

"I skin pop, so I won't know right away," he says.

Big Charlie doesn't like the fast rush of heroin in his bloodstream. Like everything else he does, he takes heroin the slow way, sliding the needle under the skin of his forearm where it will be absorbed gradually, like a nicotine patch stuck on the skin.

"It's pretty good," he says with a shrug after a while.

More lactose is added and Joe returns with a dozen of Benadryl boxes. He and his wife get busy emptying the Benadryl onto a separate plate. Once the cut has been mixed again, young Joe takes a capful of heroin to the bathroom. He comes back a few minutes later and we all look at him with expectations. But his eyes are too bright for someone who has just fixed.

"They'll like it in Prince George," he says to me with a friendly smile.

It doesn't matter. Charlie added too much cut but it all goes for the same price and next time will be better. I'm just glad that this stuff isn't likely to kill anyone.

NORM BOUCHER

It's time to cap up. The powder is spread on small plates and Charlie and Joe sit around the table, each taking a plate. They begin the night-long process of filling the tiny gelatin capsules with the powder, tapping the open ends in the pile of cut heroin so that it will pack itself inside the caps. It's long and tedious work and it takes some skill to make sure the powder stays inside the caps.

Tap, tap, tap.

After an hour, Max becomes impatient.

"You're doing it wrong," he tells Charlie. "Don't make them too tight."

The big man slowly gets up to make room for Max.

Tap, tap, tap.

Soon, the excitement is subdued by the continuing, dull hum of the caps hitting the table. After a few hours, I walk to the front window. It has been raining and the shiny wet pavement reflects the porch lights of the dormant houses across the empty street. I return to the kitchen where the capping up is still going on relentlessly.

Tap, tap, tap.

I look at these drug addicts working together, their faces hard with concentration. Everyone is tired. The teenager has come back to the kitchen and is now leaning on the counter, watching with detached interest. Joe asks him to get a bottle of baby powder from the bedroom and the kid walks off. When he returns, Joe's wife stuffs a small amount of the baby powder into the balloons so they can slide out easily when it's time to sell them. She then feeds the caps into each balloon. In no time we have nearly a couple dozen balloons, round as golf balls, each one filled with twenty-five caps and making a tight package that can be swallowed.

I pick up my six bundles and walk to the door. It's morning and daylight is filtering through the small window curtains.

"How long are you gonna be in George?" asks Max.

"Just a few days."

"When you come back, I'll show you my restaurant."

A GIRL FROM TORONTO

In every long-term operation there is a turning point where life on the street becomes easier than your home life. The hustle and the highs and lows of the heroin scene are now a part of me and have taken over everything else, dimming down everything that goes on in my personal life. Even the regular meetings with the cover team and the paperwork I need to do sitting at my desk are starting to fade as incidental interruptions from my life on the street. And the long shifts and irregular schedules make it increasingly difficult to meet the everyday demands of both my private and professional lives. There are no office meetings or water cooler chats, no bosses around, and an inability to plan anything at home or to interact openly with acquaintances and friends. To pass the day, I decide to wallpaper the walls in our townhome, but my focus isn't on it, and my wife and I now live in a permanent mess. Long operations can literally suck the life out of you, especially if you are attached. I live in the suburbs and am happy that I can do my work without having to travel. I like my job and wouldn't trade it for anything in the world. Like any other job worth doing, undercover is hard work, and it is in coming home and doing the things you like with the people you love that you get the most satisfaction. I've met undercover police officers who seem to maintain their undercover personae at home and at the office. Most of us don't. With this job, and the length of it, I leave everything on the dance floor. I like the contrast with who I am in my own personal life. This is where I get my pride. I don't talk about my work a lot, and people usually think, not without reason, that it has to do with its confidentiality. But the truth is, I don't like to talk about my workday. I just like coming home tired and getting into the routine of the day. Be myself, just as we all do. But with this operation, given its highs and lows and the length of it, it is getting increasingly difficult. A long-term undercover operation will do that.

Nonetheless, once I put on my leather jacket and make my way to the Strip, my mind is clear. And when I pull on the heavy handle of the Blackstone's front door, while wondering who's inside and who isn't and what the feel of the place will be when I get in, I may as well be a thousand miles away from home, in another life. I get nervous scheming and dealing with people I don't trust and who shouldn't trust me, but every day has its own energy and I like the dose of adrenaline I get out of it. Everything is clear and simple.

Working the street brings you down to basic needs, and when things are kept simple and hard, you know what you have to do. There's no guessing. I can grab a table in the bar and immediately get a feel for the action. The hypes of the Blackstone don't have to say much. As soon as you sit with them you know if there's heroin around. "You looking?" is all they have to say. Some of them absorb everything that goes on around them. They watch the heat come and go and they know who is working and with whom. They know when the heroin is going to arrive, who to go to for it, and who to stay away from. Captain Kangaroo is like that. I often sit with him against the wall in the Blackstone where we wait for the action to start. The old man knows where the good stuff is and he knows the rip-off artists. He never makes a fuss. He has reached an age where he can suffer quietly.

This is what they do best, the hypes, suffer quietly, and I am investing a lot of myself in keeping up with them. My first undercover job took me away from home for months, and I learned then to stay away from any relationships that do not involve the drug business, turning down personal invitations where I can, and leaving soon after the deal is done. It's easy to detach yourself when it's about money. But this is about heroin users and how their addiction suffocates every other aspect of their lives, including the business side of drugs. I need to move away from that.

Going up in the hierarchy of drug traffickers is what every operator shoots for. It's what drives us. Captain Kangaroo is getting old, and at times, the action goes by him and he doesn't chase it, so even if it is good to be seen with him, I need to go elsewhere for business. I could use Chico to find some leads, but he is beginning to look desperate. His hair and beard are getting long and he has lost the last of his front teeth in another street skirmish. I can tell that he is using again, and for some addicts, a few months are a lifetime. He is no longer someone I can count on, and I doubt that anyone else will trust him with a supply. Some heroin users will deteriorate to a bad end when there is product around, and looking at some of the Blackstone's users and dealers, I begin to realize that the regulars have very little control over their own lives. Friendship among these hypes starts and ends with heroin use and there is never any talk of getting off the drug. Like the alcoholics of the Blackstone who sit every day alone or in pairs a few tables over, the more they have, the deeper they sink.

It's time for me to move away from the daily grind of the Blackstone hypes and get into some real action. To begin, I clean up my appearance a touch more. I still wear the same clothes but keep my hair and beard trimmed, just enough to improve my image without causing someone to notice a drastic change. A few days later, when Chico comes to see me to ask again if I can put him into action, I brush him off. Later on, Maggie tells me that Harry has access to bundles, and that he wants me to buy from him. This one is easier to get away from. I remind her of the heat we took the last time we dealt together.

Jodie also wants in and asks if I want to partner with her. She is nice and makes me feel like a close friend, so it is more difficult to move away from her because I like her and she knows it. I tell her that we can talk when I return from my next trip up north. In the end, I can't be a guy with money and remain a regular in the Blackstone. It's time to show the heroin users that I have moved on to better things, that I control my own supply and my own life.

So from then on, whenever I walk into the Blackstone, I walk quickly through it as if I were looking for someone, just like the other bundle dealers do when they want to settle a score. I'm all business. And if I decide to sit for a while, I no longer talk about my own business; instead, I check out the action to see what's going on with the heat, who's putting out heroin, and who is ripping off whom. And people come to me. Not to talk about caps, but to talk bundle deals, just because I act like a bundle dealer. Even if most of these deals don't materialize, talking business with them is still the best way to feel any threat coming. I keep my fingers on the pulse, and as long as people come to me, I know that I'm okay.

Whenever Jimmy and I meet in the Blackstone, we walk together to the other bars and check out the action. After that, we usually get together with Max at the Austin where we talk drugs and money. Max's girlfriend often takes a break from her job at the hotel and joins us, but we don't talk drugs when she's around. They are engaged and speak mainly about getting married. She knows most of the hypes, but doesn't interact with them except to take messages for Max.

On a bright day in July, sitting at a table with Max, I meet

Caroline for the first time. She comes in the Austin and walks directly to our table. She is a breath of fresh air. Her straight brown hair bounces on her shoulders as she walks in to see Max and his fiancée. She has a nice smile, smooth skin with an olive tan, and dark brown eyes. Intelligent and bright, I cannot understand what she is doing with Max at the Austin.

"Where are you from?" I ask.

"Toronto. I got here a couple of weeks ago."

"Why here?"

"This is where the action is. It's a good place. I had a business in Toronto and I sold it all to come here."

"What kind of business?"

"Hair salon."

"So what do you do now?"

"I do business with Max." She grins.

"You a user?" I ask.

"I play with it."

I look at her. She looks too healthy. Her skin is too nice and her face too full to be a junkie. I imagine her walking in and out of shops on Yonge Street in her skirt and coloured tights, but I'm having difficulties seeing her shooting heroin behind the door of a smelly washroom stall.

A few days later, she is sitting with Max and his fiancée when Jimmy and I walk in the Austin. Caroline smiles at me. She has offered to do the invitations for Max's wedding and we take turn looking at the samples, picking the ones we like. Max, his fiancée, and Caroline get excited talking about the wedding preparations. For me, this is a time where I am merely a spectator, knowing that this side of me doesn't really exist, even if I take part in the chats. I often take advantage of these moments to listen in and take a good look at my targets, noting their scars and tattoos, sometime chatting about where they live and when they are born, to help me later when I am sitting in the witness box. Evidence aside, during these bursts of casual conversations, I can look at people and interact with them with the impartiality of someone about to leave town. Sitting in the Austin with Max and the others, it's easy to forget the conversations I have across the street in the Blackstone, where everyone at my table is either sick and waiting, or on the nod.

Whenever a drug dealer makes money it brings on an instinctive urge to show it off. To that end, I take Jimmy aside and invite him and Selina to have dinner with me. Jimmy introduced me to Max and he is willing to work with me on the score in Prince George. I owe him and it makes sense for me to show my gratitude, and build some trust to keep him on side. Drug dealers are impulsive people and when they score some decent money, they spend big in expensive places. My initial idea is to take them to a nice, expensive place to let him know that I am now making good money hoping that he and Selina can pass the word around. The problem is that someone in the RCMP can't relate to the contradictions of street life so they give me sixty bucks to take Jimmy and Selina out for dinner. I know that this could hurt me at the end, but the three of us jump into my car and drive to Mr. Jake, a cafeteria-style restaurant, where we pick up our trays and line up in front of the different dishes of food, picking up our drinks along with assorted stews, fried chicken, and pasta.

"Take what you want," I say, feeling like an actor stuck in a bad movie.

Being cheap is now part of my story and they will dislike me for it, but for now, Jimmy and Selina are good with me, even thanking me when I drop them off. They're actually nice people when you take the street out of them.

In the following days, I spread the word that I am not using anymore. It will be a break from the one or two-cap habit routine this undercover job called for when I started. I know that people on the street will not totally believe it, but I also know that everybody lies about how much they use. It's the thing to do. Just like Caroline saying that she only "plays with it," bragging that she controls her habit instead of the other way around, I let people know that I'm on top of my game.

When I see Max again in the Austin, I take him aside. "How's the restaurant coming along?"

"Good, you want to go see it?"

"Yeah, I'm thinking of getting into something myself."

Max's restaurant is in a small house on the North Shore. It sits on a hill above the secluded green shores of Deep Cove. It has a real West Coast feel, with its cedar siding and large windows. The street itself is narrow and meanders among tall cedars on the side of a mountain, overlooking Indian Arm. The humid air smells of pine and burning firewood.

Restaurants are a good way to launder money, but it is only recently that money laundering became a law enforcement concern. There is a unit in the office called "Proceeds of Crimes," but the laws are new and untested in court, and no one knows how it is going to work in the long run. At any given time, there are a dozen policemen hovering around the heroin addicts of the Blackstone, but no one is looking at Max's restaurant. Yet, money is what this is really all about.

To the public, there's nothing like a team of policemen kicking a door and showing bags of white powder on television. People can relate to that. Over fifty years have passed since Al Capone was taken down by the profit side of the law, and society is still looking at it as if it was an anomaly. Even then, smashing barrels of booze made for great news stories compared to an accountant sitting at a desk. A display of drugs and guns sitting on a table makes for great television compared to boxes of fiscal documents amassed over months of desk work. Max will go to jail for selling heroin, but he will likely keep his restaurant. It's a lot easier to take a drug dealer's freedom away than to take his assets.

Max likes the idea of dealing with someone he can trust, someone who doesn't use.

"I've got a connection for a quarter ounce of pure, better than last time. You want in?"

"Yeah, but not like last time. Too many people were involved, and all the leaving the house to get caps. I didn't like that. I do my own capping."

"I know ...I know. This time is different."

"Plus, if I put up half the money, I want half of it," I continue. "I want what I pay for."

"Listen, you keep your eight ball and I keep my stuff. This is a new guy, he only wants to deal with a couple of people. He doesn't want to deal with the hypes. I'll tell him you're good and we can meet him together."

"Give me a few days to put my money together." I shake his hand. "And let's make this steady, just you and me."

SUNRISE

As usual, East Hastings is busy. While most crowded areas attract people because they are everyone's first choice, the Skids are busy because it's everyone's last resort. In that grungy strip of dilapidated buildings, good heroin is hard to find, but sex, pills, and chemical drugs are everywhere and you don't have to look too hard. Whenever someone goes to the Skids, with money or not, it's because they are desperate for something, and for many, it's the end of the line.

If the West Coast is the destination of choice for all of the transients from across the country, the Downtown Eastside is the end of the road for those who didn't make it. Dealers and scammers always look for the new faces and in a way it's easier to get in than on the Granville Strip. The trick is not to get ripped.

The Sunrise is packed and I decide to try my luck there first. Unlike the Brandiz, where street deals seem to make the atmosphere heavy, the Sunrise is a wide-open romp with everyone drunk or stoned, yelling, laughing, and shaking hands.

"Are you looking for pot?" asks an Indigenous youth.

"I'm looking for something else," I say.

"What you looking for?"

"H."

"I'll look around for you. I'm Danny. Here, sit here with my friends."

Two guys are sitting with a young girl at a table covered with glasses of beer, some full and some empty. One of the guys, well in his forties, pushes a glass of beer toward me.

"Stay a while," he says with a smile. "There's nothing to do out there."

He has a face full of creases and folds arranged in a jovial pattern that suggest he would laugh all the way to his grave, no matter what. We chat in a friendly way and the girl stays quiet. She nurses her beer and seems to enjoy listening to the conversation without getting involved in it.

After a short while, Danny comes back and says that he found someone across the street who could help me. We walk across to Brandiz, but can't find his connection, so we return to the Sunrise. It has filled up even more with a great number of street rounders in smoky mackinaws and greasy jean jackets. I sit next to the girl. Danny asks me to buy him a beer and, not minding being used a little while he looks around, I order a round. He takes a swig and leaves again. The older man takes the beer. The girl doesn't touch hers.

"Thanks," the man says amicably, clinking glasses with me, "you didn't have to."

"I don't mind. I like this place, plus Danny is helping me out."

"Hope it works out," he says.

"Well, if it doesn't work out, I'm still in the black. I'm having a good time."

We clink glasses again and the other man joins in.

I take a swallow of the beer and smile at the girl. "How about you, are you having a good time?"

The girl smiles timidly. Two more guys come in and sit with us. They are happy and loud and we all shake hands.

"Where's Danny?" one of them asks.

"He's doing some errands," the old man says.

"He's always doing errands ...always got something big going."

"Yeah and never has any money," the other one says and they all laugh.

More beer comes and we chat for a while. Danny comes and goes, but nothing is happening. I buy another round, and after Danny comes back a couple of times, the girl puts her hand on my arm.

"You should be careful with him," she says. "He's getting drunk."

"Do you know him?"

"No, I just met him today."

The girl and I chat and I learn that she is from Williams Lake and has no family in Vancouver.

"I just got out of jail," she says.

"Then we can celebrate," I say, clinking my glass to hers, the beer getting flat on the table.

I don't ask why she was in jail. She says that she is glad to be out, but her face doesn't say so. It doesn't say anything.

"Where do you live?" she asks.

"Burnaby. What about you?"

"I don't know yet."

"You shouldn't be here," I say after a while. "You just got out and this isn't a good place for you."

"I have no place to stay tonight," she says again. "I have nowhere to go."

"Do you want to call someone?"

"No," she says, shaking her head, "I'm just tired."

I turn my attention to the bar. She is just one of the many who have no place to go.

"It doesn't look like it's working out with Danny."

"I like you," she says. "You need to be careful with him."

She brings her face close to mine and kisses me. It's a sweet kiss and I like it and she knows it.

"We should go somewhere else," she says, her face still close to mine.

"I can't, I have to wait for Danny and then I have to go."

Danny comes back and sits with us.

"How did you make out?" I ask.

"There's nothing around."

"I've been here a long time waiting, man."

"Yeah, and there's nothing around. I've been looking around for you and I get nothing out of it." Danny glances at the girl. "I don't even fucking know you," he continues.

I take a sip of my beer. "Yeah, thanks for trying."

"Where you from?" he asks.

Danny's sudden interest brings on the attention of the others.

"I'm out in Burnaby," I reply.

"Who do you know here?"

"I don't come here much."

One of the newly arrived guys is staring at me. "I saw his horse parked outside," he says.

The guy is calling me a Mountie, but I decide to leave it. Sensing the turn in the conversation, the old guy gets up.

"He's okay. He's okay," he says, giving me a pat on the shoulder before leaving.

Danny takes the now empty seat next to the girl, drapes his arm around the back of her chair and stares at me. The girl stares ahead, silent.

"What are you doing here?" he asks.

"I was out on Granville and there's nothing right now, but forget about it. I don't need anything from you."

I stand up and walk out of the Sunrise without looking back at the girl.

CONNECTING WITH CAROLINE

They say undercover operators aren't actors, that they are role players. They say that, unlike actors, we retain our own personality, but only pretend to be on a different path in our lives. Being an actor would make my job easier because I would detach myself completely from what I do and see. Even when I try to detach myself and concentrate on the drug suppliers, my job keeps bringing me back to the Blackstone and the Skids. Too many people get hurt in these places. And I like some of them.

I think about the girl at the Sunrise and wonder where she is now. I haven't seen Angie since the night she sat silently at my side before walking away alone to turn tricks on Main Street. Seeing Chico turning into a street addict bothers me, but I should not involve myself. My job is to stay on my path, nothing more.

I walk through the Blackstone and see the dealers against the wall. They are users before anything else, and now that they know me, and believe that I have my own heroin connections, I don't need to spend as much time with them every day. I know that Chico is angry that I don't want to deal with him, but he and the other users can no longer hurt me now that I am connected. That's the thing with users, they are powerless against anyone who has a supply, unless they decide to talk to the cops, and I'm not worried about that. I'm moving on.

"Selina and I are on the juice," Jimmy announces one night, referring to the methadone program, where on each visit you receive a small cup of orange juice laced with methadone.

Selina smiles.

"We're moving to North Van," she says.

"That's great," I say. "Will you still be around?"

"Yeah, yeah, we'll keep coming down."

I'm not sure how moving to the suburbs will work for them, but I'm glad to see their excitement.

While Jimmy and Selina are trying to move away from heroin, Caroline spends a lot of time getting deeper into it. Like me, she hangs around Max, but she also has her own independent heroin connections. There is an attitude about her that fits nicely with how I operate, and you can almost believe that she plays with heroin and not the other way around. It's as if you were to pick up a bright businesswoman and drop her right in the middle of Vancouver's heroin scene, telling her to go out there and play. She understands the game well, and is already well connected to some of the known traffickers. She does it all with a smile.

"I hear that you're going up north," she says on one quiet afternoon.

"Who told you that?"

"I have my sources."

"I don't go there anymore," I say knowing that she will see this as a lie.

"I can help you."

I don't pursue it and soon, several people come to our table, people I know and some I don't. They are attracted to Caroline.

She doesn't look like a user and her smile will brighten up your mood on any bad day. Unlike the other women I meet, she doesn't work under any man and seems free and independent. But she is also hungry. She wants action as much as I do, and it's impressive to see what a driven, talented, and attractive woman can do when she wants her fix.

Max and his fiancée come to our table and we chat a while. Caroline is almost done with the calligraphy of their wedding invitations and is passing the new samples around the table. The samples look good and everyone is excited and talking about the wedding.

I'm not interested in Caroline's wedding invitations, but I need to know about her heroin connection. I take Caroline aside.

"You said you could help me?"

"What do you need?"

"I need to do four Bs real quick."

"Let me make a phone call."

Caroline comes back within a few minutes. "He has it. I can do it for eighteen hundred. Give me the money and I'll get it."

"I don't want to front my money. I have to go with you."

"He won't like it if I bring you."

"I'll drop you off a block away if you want."

Caroline takes a deep breath and looks away.

"Don't let him see you," she says, now looking me in the eyes.

"I'll get my money."

An hour later, I pick up Caroline in front of the Austin and we take Kingsway all the way to New Westminster. Kingsway cuts through the north-south streets in an angle, like the slash of a greasy pen on graph paper. It is one of those early major arteries that, decades before, travelled directly from New West to the city centre and around which north-south city streets were later built.

Caroline puts her hand behind my headrest and makes me feel like we're a couple.

"You know, I've got some good connections in Toronto, if you want to make some real money."

"How long would it take you to arrange something?"

"Just a phone call."

I say that I am interested and we talk prices, Caroline giving me the figures and me nodding my head, both feeling good about what this partnership could mean to us.

"It's the one there on the left," she says as we pass a fairly new and well-maintained high-rise apartment building.

I drive by the building and then stop half a block away where I give Caroline the money. She walks to a man at the front entrance of the apartment. I can see in my rear-view mirror that he seems agitated. He talks to her and then walks out near the street to better look in all directions. I can see that he knows what he's doing because he is scared. He has his head on a swivel and tries to take in everything, like a small animal in an open field. That's what it takes to be a good trafficker. You have to be scared.

I know now that Caroline has pushed the deal on him. This isn't a set thing. She pushed him with her smarts and good looks and he is now suspicious. I also know that buying from Caroline will bring me heat at the Austin. I have a good thing going with Max and there's no need to go and do business with her.

Caroline comes back and gives me the four Bs. "I told you I could do it!"

"I believed you," I say, stuffing the heroin into my boot.

"Can you spare a few off the top?" she asks, "as a tip?"

"I'd like to, but it's all committed. I have to take the whole thing to George tonight."

There is silence and I know that the addict in her had counted on it.

"I could go with you to Prince George," she says with a faint smile, her dark brown eyes full of promise.

"Another time, maybe."

We drive back, immersed in traffic. Caroline looks ahead without a word. As we approach the downtown core the Lions Mountains, dark and untamed, watch over us, making the silence heavy.

I drop Caroline off at the Austin and head to the Shack where I fill the cover team in on the Toronto deal.

"We did some checks on her," says one of the cover men. "She used to live in Toronto," he continues. "The Sergeant over there tells me that she owned a hair salon. Her sister got in with the wrong crowd and started to do heroin. She got involved with them to help her sister get out and she started using herself ...lost everything ...had to leave town."

"She's connected, but I don't know if she can work in Toronto anymore," says Smitty.

"She seems to like you," a cover man says with a wink.

"Yeah, we get along."

JIMMY GIVES ME HEAT

A few days later, I am eager to go to the Austin to meet Jimmy. He said on the telephone that it's important. To me, this means that he has some kind of action, possibly a new connection. It may also be that he wants in on my action with Max.

Looking forward to a new deal, I look for him at the usual tables in the bar area. He isn't there, so I check the lounge, which is usually empty at that time of day. Jimmy is sitting alone in a far corner, smoking a cigarette and facing the door. I am happy to find him there, but he stares at me hard as I walk in.

"I could kill you," he says.

I pull up a chair and see in his eyes that he means it.

"I could kill you," he repeats as I sit down.

"What are you talking about?" I ask.

"People are saying things about you," he says, his eyes still fixated on mine, looking for a sign.

The way he is sitting, alone against the wall, leaning back in his chair, I know that he has stewed about this for a while.

"You're going around buying from everybody and nobody knows you," he continues.

"You know me," I say with a shrug.

"I don't fucking know you! I did a deal with you. That's all I know."

"Yeah and it's going good between you and me. What the fuck, you know me ...who you gonna listen to?"

"Good? And what am I gonna get out of this? Another fucking dinner at Mr. Jake!"

The friend in Jimmy has opened a door for me. If it's to be about money, I have to make up a story before things breaks down further.

"It's up to you, man. We both don't need this. If you don't trust me, I'll just go my own way. We don't need this you and me," I say, shaking my head. "You gonna listen to them or you gonna listen to me?"

"I don't like what I'm hearing," Jimmy says.

"Listen, I wanted to talk to you about a score in George," I continue. "It's a good score, but if you don't feel good about it don't worry about it."

"I'm listening."

"I know where there's a safe. There's over a hundred grand, but I got to wait till somebody goes on holidays. There's a person I want out of the way before I can do anything...."

Jimmy nods as if he knows what I am talking about.

"...Then we get in. I got somebody inside knows how to get in. The thing is ...I need to get the money out of George and bring it back here and I can't do it alone. Somebody I can trust. It's a lot of money and I need somebody solid. I'm too well known over there and I may have some heat on me, so I'll have to be away until things cool off."

"I can bring the money back," Jimmy offers, crushing his cigarette in the ashtray. "I'm not known in George."

Jimmy is in on the deal, but I know that the heat is creeping up as sure and slow as the tides of the Pacific a few blocks away. To keep going I would need extra money from the RCMP to pull more elaborate scams, but they have already shown me that the money isn't there. Like Chico before him, Jimmy was straight with me when he said people didn't trust me, but a day will come when he won't talk to me, and I'll have to watch for that.

"Great. I'll let you know when it's time. For now, I got to finish my deal with Max and get back to George so I can set things up."

We shake hands hard and high, Jimmy holding my hand for a solid beat while looking at me in the eyes.

Walking through the Austin, I see Max and walk up to him. I want to see if the heat came from him, so I can do some damage control.

"How's it going?"

"Good," Max says. "You ready?"

"Yeah, I just did a decent score ...got my money together."

"Thirty-six hundred for an eighth of pure," he says, "your own ...and it's good ...even better than last time."

It looks like Max isn't the one saying things about me.

FRED

The next day, Max and I leave in my car to meet his new connection. This is a real step up for me, a quarter of an ounce of "pure" heroin for $3,600. They call it pure on the street, but like any heroin sold in packages less than a pound, I know that it has already been stepped on. Still, the yield is better than a street ounce, which for $5,000 would have given me forty grams, or about sixteen to twenty bundles of three to four per cent heroin. Max isn't putting up any money up front, and he needs me to do the deal. All of his cash has gone into his restaurant.

"I'm getting a gram and a half on the cuff," he says as we get on our way, "but the Man's pissed because it took you so long to get your money together. He's connected, you know. We don't want to fuck with him."

We stop at a townhouse in a trendy West End neighbourhood and I am prepared to face the heat.

"You told him to have it there, didn't you? Already split up for you and me," I ask Max before getting out of the car.

"Yeah, yeah, he will," he assures me. "He's good for it."

We climb a short set of stairs to the lower floor of the cedar-sided condo building. An elderly man opens the door. He is tall and bald except for a thin layer of short white hair encircling his head. He has an affable way about him, enhanced by a pair of chequered pants and a cardigan. He holds the door open with a firm grip, leaning slightly forward and smiling like a grandfather welcoming the family. We walk past him to the back of the apartment and sit at the kitchen table.

Fred is well into his sixties. He speaks gently, throwing in a pause once in a while to get his thoughts together.

"Would you like some coffee?" he asks.

"No, thank you," I say.

"Milk?"

"Sure, milk is good."

Fred takes glasses out of the cupboards and fills them with milk. He puts oatmeal cookies on a small plate and brings them to the table along with the two glasses of milk.

"I don't have to go get it. The guy trusts me," he says.

"You have it separate?" I ask.

"Yes. One for Max and one for you."

"I've been looking for a steady supply," I say, "something reliable so I don't have to look every time."

"I need good people," Fred replies. "I don't want to deal with people like Harry and the rest. I don't need all that heat. I just want to work with the same steady people ...good people."

"That's exactly what we need," Max says.

Fred goes to the back of the fridge and pulls out two packages wrapped in cellophane. He gives the bigger of the two to me.

"What's the percentage?" I ask, dipping my cookie into the cold milk.

"It'll be in the eighties. It comes from California, they don't step on it over there."

"I'm gonna check the percentage and the weight before we do any more deals. Did you weigh it yourself?"

Fred gives me a serious look over. I've insulted him.

"You won't have any problems," he says.

I examine my package. The material is tightly packed and hard, taped and wrapped in cellophane and toilet paper. I cut into my package. The powder is the colour of cream, silky. Fred doesn't talk like a salesman and I believe him when he says that it's good.

"You have the money? I have to go pay the guy."

I give Fred the cash.

"Don't leave until I get back," Fred says walking away.

With Fred gone, Max looks at the two packages of heroin sitting in front of me. "You're getting it at nine hundred a gram. I'm paying a thousand, but that's because I'm getting it on the cuff."

Max opens his package and sticks his finger in it. He licks a tiny amount of the powder and smiles.

I have no doubt that Fred is taking his time walking around the block and checking for heat on his way to meet his supplier. He returns about fifteen minutes later.

"You going to the races tomorrow?" Max asks Fred.

"Yes."

Fred retrieves a folded newspaper from the kitchen counter. He pulls reading glasses from his shirt pocket and looks over the race sheet. He and Max discuss some of the horses and their odds.

"Fred did time in Alcatraz," Max says to me.

"Really? Did you know the bird man?" I ask Fred, half joking.

Fred raises his eyes from the newspaper and looks at me over his glasses. "Yes, but in that movie, they didn't show it right. It wasn't like that. I spent fifteen years in Alcatraz," he continues, "before they moved me to Sing Sing. I was on death row twice."

Max is smiling. "Show him your papers," he tells Fred with excitement.

Fred walks out of the kitchen and returns with a cigar box filled with papers yellowed by time. He pulls two typewritten letters and examines them as if to make sure they still say what they are supposed to, and passes them to me. The letterheads are in the name of Sing Sing and his name is in the headings. They are religious statements written in the form of personal letters to the authorities in which Fred speaks of the time he spent alone in his cell in Alcatraz, waiting to be executed, and how it has affected his connection with the world. He speaks of how important it is to help and support others who are in need and how his faith in God has helped him see things in a different light. He speaks of life itself as a gift and of his strong desire to give back and he speaks of the people who have helped him get through over twenty years of jail time. He is a new man and is thankful for it.

"We had to do it if we wanted parole," he says as he watches me read the statements. "The parole people even sent someone to help us write it."

The writing is so convincing that I feel inspired by it, and even if it was done to deceive the Parole Board, there is an irrevocable truth to the words. Looking at Fred, old and deferential, I can only begin to imagine how he views the world. Over his adult life, he has spent more time in jail than as a free man.

I look at the drugs sitting on the table and wonder why a man of his age chose to continue in this lifestyle. He's already spent a good chunk of his life in jail and you'd think that he would be inclined to take it easy and find a straight job somewhere, living a quiet life away from heroin, maybe stocking shelves at the grocery store or running the cash at the gas station.

Max and I get up and I stuff my package into the lining of my boot. As we walk by his bedroom, Fred stops and takes us inside.

"I want to show you something," he says.

Laid out on the bed are a number of Polaroid pictures of a young woman posing in her underwear.

"This girl used to come here all the time," he says, not without pride.

The pictures were taken on the bed they are now resting on. She appears to be in her early twenties and, by the tone of her skin and her slight, bony frame, a heroin user. She is posing teasingly, but her eyes look tired and on the nod even as she smiles for the camera. Fred picks up one of the pictures and passes it to me.

"Good-looking girl," I say.

"Yes, she was ...very sweet girl,"

"What happened to her?"

"She died of an overdose.... I told her she was using too much."

I give back the photo and Fred contemplates it. I don't know what goes through his mind, but I understand then that he will not be stocking shelves at the corner store soon.

MONEY

Money. You can smell it in the air whenever we get together at the Austin where Fred will meet us, tall and distinguished, in his checkered wool sports jacket and Ascot cap. I learned from the cover team that, as a young man, he accidentally shot and killed his own partner during a botched holdup in California, serving his time in both Alcatraz and Sing Sing. That was the end of his life as a free man. Of his sixty-odd years, Fred has spent almost forty years behind bars. Being a Canadian citizen, he was eventually allowed to come back to Vancouver to finish his sentence. He is still on parole, which explains why he stays away from the other street dealers and never sets foot inside the Blackstone.

Like many old-timers in the heroin business, Fred loves the horse races. To him, the track is a good place to connect with the old crowd of career drug traffickers and jail pals with names that come up in police files time and time again. Colourful names like "Cadillac Red," "Freddy Munster," and "the Plumber" show up in debriefing reports along with names of Chinese, Indian, or Eastern European origin.

These names are a part of Vancouver's underground history and they are often mentioned by informants in the back of unmarked police cars, when a new shipment of heroin has arrived, or when a street dealer is found dead in an alley. All of these old-timers know each other, the police know them, and informants talk about them. They are gamblers before anything else, always looking for a bigger score. They aren't organized like the gangs of Montréal, but have a more open, West Coast attitude where everyone can get his piece of the action and no one has control. They play cards together in illegal gambling joints and meet at the track. Some are heavy users of heroin, but you would never know it because they've learned to live and work with it.

These old-timers have also learned the hard way that a good dose of paranoia is the only way to make a business out of drug dealing. They never leave home without looking out for the heat, and even when they are clean, they drive around an extra block before settling for the night. They may get worn out from the game, but like gambling, it's a part of their lives and they will never leave it. Fred is my only connection to these old-timers, but they never come down to the Austin and I can't go the track because, unlike the Granville Strip, the race track is a place where I could easily encounter people who know me as a policeman. After they have gone to the races, Max, Jimmy, and Fred usually sit in the Austin lounge with Max's wife, Selina, and Caroline where, unlike the Blackstone, the money is what binds us together.

I still claim that I no longer use, but once in a while I take Jimmy with me to score a cap from one of the Blackstone dealers. It makes Jimmy feel good to hear me tell someone that I don't use when he knows that it isn't true and that I'm still chipping. The complicity makes us feel like we can trust each other. When I decide to go back to Stan for a cap Jimmy stays at my side.

"I don't have anything," Stan says as he did before.

Jimmy goes to him and grabs the sleeve of his jacket. "He's okay."

"Yeah, yeah, no problem. How many do you want."

I sit next to Stan. "Just one."

Stan spits the bundle into his hand and does the deal.

I immediately leave as if I needed to fix, and after giving it enough time, I meet Jimmy and the others again at the Austin, where I have now become a regular. Only across the street from the Blackstone, the Austin is really a world away. It's filled with patrons of every sorts, businessmen and delivery men, some on a break with their company's logo embroidered on their shirts, all there to see the strippers. The Austin looks good. It has redone its walls, added some lights, and a Mexican food buffet was installed near the windows. You could live there.

IT'S JUST BUSINESS

I load my taco shells with the sloppy mixture of spicy ground beef and top them off with the fresh, crisp trimmings. In the early months of the operation, I got used to being hungry, living at the pace of heroin users, walking back and forth from the Austin, to the St. Helen's, and then to the Blackstone, always looking for action or following someone looking for action. A meal with the hypes is usually a piece of fried chicken at Jerry's Café around midnight, a few hours after their fix so they are no longer on the nod. Since I'm no longer following their routine, I can sit alone in the Austin and eat the filled tacos, picking up the dropped trimmings clean from the plate.

After the meal, I walk over to the lounge where I see Selina sitting at a table across from an older man. He is leaning forward talking to her intimately and she looks at him as if there is no one else in the world. A few tables over, Jimmy is sitting with Max and a couple guys I don't know. I walk by Selina and take a seat at Jimmy's table.

"Look at her work," Jimmy says with pride, pointing his chin at Selina and her john.

The man speaks softly and you can tell that he cares about her.

"This guy's in the oil business ...from up north," Jimmy adds as we both watch, "...comes here a couple times a year."

"You got a good girl, man," I say, clinking his glass.

The man takes Selina's hand into his. He has a weathered, but gentle face and a worker's hands.

"He has her for the whole weekend," Jimmy says, "pays good money."

Jimmy and Selina act every day like any working couple. They care for each other and have a stable relationship. Selina is a user and a prostitute, but she doesn't get into any other illegal activity. She is honest, reliable, and when she is with Jimmy they talk about normal things: shopping, eating at restaurants, and paying the bills. But they are both hard street people and when it's time to earn money for their fix, they do what they have to. Selina's money pays for the rent, food, and the drugs they inject into their arms. All Jimmy has to do is sit back and talk about his next score. There is always a next score, a bigger score. Looking at her stroking her client's arm, I wonder how far Jimmy would go, whether there are rules for guys who pimp their girlfriends.

Before long, Serge the Gastown weed dealer comes in with his two girlfriends, Melanie and Daniela, and I am glad to see them. I like the girls. They are pretty, friendly, and a good break from the prostitutes and drug fiends of the Blackstone scene. Weed is a social drug and Serge is always cool about things. The three of them are close together and they don't need to talk a lot to understand each other. We help the waiter pull a few tables together and I order a round.

"What would you like?" I ask the girls.

They look at Serge and hesitate.

"Anything!" I insist.

I turned to the waiter. "Make it a surprise ...put some colour into it, like fruit or something."

Serge and the two girls are sitting across from Jimmy and me, with Max and his two friends at the end of the table. Soon the drinks come, two Singapore Slings for the girls and beer for the rest of us, and we order a few plates of chicken wings. This is going to be that kind of night and I feel like I need it. Nothing to do with buying drugs, a night to chat, and laugh, and drink.

Everyone soon begins to feel good. Max talks about the restaurant he is setting up and everyone agrees that Deep Cove is a beautiful location for it.

"We're gonna do something for the opening. I want all you guys to come for the opening."

We drink to that.

Jimmy glances at Selina and tells everyone that he plans to buy a new stereo with the money she is earning with her weekend date.

"The guy's loaded," he says.

We drink to that.

Meanwhile, the two guys are getting pretty drunk and they are hitting on the girls. The girls laughed it off, and sip their drinks. We don't talk drugs and it's a nice change. The rest of the lounge is empty except for Selina and her client and another table or two, and it feels like a private get-together. I sit back and listen to the two guys at the end of the table teasing each other about a bad bet one of them made at the horse races.

Whack!

I wasn't looking, but I heard it and everyone is now quiet. Serge is standing and staring down at Melanie, who is still sitting, her head leaning forward. He is shaking. His face is red and I can see his pulse in the veins of his neck. His arm is bent and his fist closed.

"Don't you fucking do that again," he says, his eyes fixed on her.

Whack!

The sound of bone hitting bone. Serge hits Melanie in full

force again with a closed fist on her cheek. Her head wavers and she keeps her eyes down in front of her. Blood trickles out of her mouth, and falls in long strings onto her lap. Serge is still shaking and his fist is still closed at his side, his elbow bent, his demented stare focused on Melanie. The table has gone quiet, waiting.

"Hey! Take it easy," I say, looking at him.

Serge turns his head and looks back at me. He is pondering my interruption—wondering if it is a challenge or if I'm on his side. We look at each other and he begins to slowly relax and to lower his fist. He is still standing, looking at me when Jimmy interrupts.

"Don't get involved, Nick." And then to Serge, "Give her another one!"

Serge winds up his fist.

Whack!

Another hit on the side of her face. Melanie is now dizzy, and if the second punch made the blood pour out of her, the third brings out the tears. She sits there sobbing and bleeding quietly.

The old guy from the oil rigs gets up, but Selina holds him back. It's business. Serge sits back down and we finish our drinks.

Later on that night, I crank the music loud while driving over the Port Mann Bridge on my way home. To my left, the quiet, dark hills of Port Coquitlam are peppered with the porch lights of sleeping houses. I slam the steering wheel of my car with both hands. I don't feel good. It's not natural to sit and watch someone being hurt. I knew when I took this heroin job that I would be getting into the grime of the junk scene, but Serge isn't even into heroin, and this wasn't about a needle in the arm. Like the grime of all drug trafficking, it was about the dirty money and what people will do to protect it.

People get hurt every day and as a cop you get to do something about it. That's why I joined the RCMP in the first place and I'd like to think that this is what I'm doing with this job. But I can still hear Jimmy tell Serge to "give her another one" and watching, while Jimmy egged him on—like the crowd at a stoning would, I guess. She had fucked with the profits and we all accepted what that meant.

GREY WHALE

The next day, about an hour's drive from the Blackstone, a cover man and I untie the sailboat at the end of the pier. Sailing is a nice way to get away from it all, so we made it a regular habit to go to White Rock, and take a co-op boat out for the day. The wind is blowing the right way. Instead of using the small outboard engine, we let the mainsail take us out quietly to the open waters of Semiahmoo Bay. With nothing but blue water around us—and Orcas Island showing its purple, rounded back in the distance—we raise the jib, trim the sheets tight, and feel the waves slap against the bow. Sailing can be busy if you work to get the most out of your sails. We work hard under a fifteen-knot wind to get that feel you get on a hard tack, the waves slapping the front of your boat while the wind stretches the sails out to the side. I smell the air, feel the wind on my face, and it's as if I am part of it.

The blue water on the horizon is throwing flashes of silver at us when we first see it: the grey back of a whale breaking water. It disappears as soon as we see it and we sit silent, looking all around us until, far on the other side of the boat, it breaks the surface again, this time showing its marvellous tail flukes.

"Coming about!" I yell as we begin our chase of the grey whale. It comes out to spout water again on four occasions, just as beautiful every time. And each time we work our sails, coming about, adjusting the main again, and hoping for a better look. But our small sailboat is no match for her, and the whale finally disappears for good far away. It has shared with us for a brief moment the waters of the bay, and we are grateful for it.

Later on that evening I park in the empty lot behind Theo's. I am nicely tired, the way you get after being out in the sun and wind all day. The sun has begun to set and the action is about to begin in the Blackstone, so I avoid getting into meaningless chatter at Theo's, and walk directly down the alley to Davie Street where, turning around the corner, I feel the still, cool air against the sun-soaked skin of my face. It seems like the world stands still in this quietly darkening hour, before the night sets in. I look ahead and see Captain Kangaroo walking toward the Blackstone.

I can tell by his quick pace that he is looking to get his fix. We talk a lot, many days each week, but I never hear him say anything about what he does during the day. I try to imagine where he is walking from. No grass to cut, or leaky faucets, or complaints about the fucking price of gas. For him, life starts with that walk to the Blackstone, if he can score. For me, this hour of the day is giving me the best feelings on earth and it doesn't owe me anything. Just like after a full day riding my horse, the mare keeping me in line, reacting to my mood until I smarten up, and grow strong and steady with her; or after a day rock climbing, kayaking, or scuba diving with a group of friends, my muscles spent, and all of the cares of the world gone, the still cool air like a pat on the back, telling me to enjoy life. Then, nothing can be better than a glass of wine under the cooling sun, and good company. This is how I feel on that afternoon, after a full day sailing. The sun and wind have left their mark on me and it would be nice to talk about it over a good meal with friends. But this isn't going to happen tonight.

Kangaroo is hurried, hunched over, and his shoulders are up as if he were fighting a cold wind. I run across to meet him. He didn't see me coming so he jumps sideways, staring at me.

"I thought you were the heat," he says with a faint smile. "You got colour on your face."

"I fell asleep on the beach."

We both walk into the Blackstone and Captain Kangaroo takes a seat at his usual table along the wall. I spot Jimmy sitting with Victor at a table nearby.

"I'll see you later," I say, leaving Kangaroo to his business.

While Jimmy is in a jovial mood, Victor gives me his usual cold shoulder.

"I found you a piece," Jimmy says. "We can go now."

"Let's take my car."

After my first deal with Max, the cover team replaced my old, beat-up Datsun with a used Monte Carlo. It's white, has an eight-track player, and the interior smells of cigar smoke. It's not a great car for undercover work, but I can fit it into my story.

"New car," Jimmy says, taking a seat.

"I need a good car for the long drives."

We drive to Kitsilano to meet Jimmy's contact. The guy doesn't answer the door until he sees Jimmy through the window. He opens the door a crack.

"Hey Jimmy! I saw the car and thought you were the heat."

"Yeah, no sweat, we're here for the piece."

"Sorry, man, but I don't have it anymore. Somebody picked it up."

The man stays in the door, blocking the way.

"That's not good, just wish you would've called me," Jimmy says.

The guy glances at me. "I didn't know you still wanted it."

"I know the fucker has it," Jimmy says as we drive away. "He just got spooked because of the car."

"Don't worry about it," I say.

Back in the Blackstone, we meet Victor again and Jimmy flashes a thick wad of bills to pay for a round. Selina comes by and Jimmy smiles at her.

"We're going out for dinner tonight," he tells her.

Selina doesn't sit down. "I can't. He wants me around until Thursday."

"That's not what the deal was."

"He's paying for it."

"Tell him you're gonna see him after dinner."

Selina sits next to Jimmy and gives him some money.

"I'm keeping some aside for the furniture," she says.

"We can talk about it."

"I've made up my mind," she says resolutely.

Jimmy is annoyed, but he smiles and she gives him a kiss.

"I have to go if I want to be back for dinner," she says with a quick wave of her hand at the table before leaving.

I lean into Jimmy. "I'm looking for a cap, anybody got?"

Jimmy turns to Victor.

"I don't know anything about it," Victor says, looking me in the eyes and shaking his head more than he needs to. I know that Victor is one of the people saying things about me. I don't like him and he doesn't trust me, so I know that I will need to work on him to fix things, but I am tired and I save it for later. We drink beer and talk about the good money there is up north. Victor wants to know what I do up there.

"I know some good people," I say.

I know that I'm spreading myself thin between the Blackstone and Max. I am pushing myself on people, going after too many things, too quick, and my stories are thinning out. Victor is inquisitive and cold and I can see him building a case against me when I'm not around. Both he and Jimmy are hustlers, managing their girl-friends' street work, one a hooker and the other a heroin trafficker. But Victor is smarter than the rest. Looking at his girlfriend and the way she dresses, I know that she deals only with people on the personal level. People she knows who have day jobs and who live in solid, old houses in Kitsilano or in nice downtown apartments. People on their way to addiction, but not yet totally there, as well as others who have settled into it. Victor doesn't trust me any more than he trusts the other Blackstone hypes. He may be slime, but he's streetwise and I respect him for that. I can hear Jimmy saying it again on that day in the lounge of the Austin: "People are saying things about you." I need to keep Victor close to me.

Later on in the evening, Jimmy and Selina take me to Fresgo for a meal. I scan the place as soon as we walk in to make sure I don't see any faces I know from my other life. I take a seat against the wall where I can keep an eye on the door.

"We've got to talk about this deal in George," I tell Jimmy while wrestling a messy burger. "The guy's gonna go away on holiday sometime in August and we need to be ready, if you're still inter-ested. Need to bring the money down."

"No problem. I've been thinking about it. Selina will bring the money down. It's a good job for a girl. She won't bring any heat on her."

After the meal, I drop them off on Davie Street and make my way to the Blackstone, where I sit with Captain Kangaroo who has already scored and is under a steady nod. I look at him, gone in his special place, his body merely a breathing machine. In an hour, we'll be chatting again and by tomorrow he'll be back into it, selling it for his own fix.

A girl named Karen comes to the table and sits with us. She has strikingly long, blond hair, which she pulls back into a tight pony-tail. Small and slim, she always wears a short black leather jacket and no makeup. Her girlfriend is with her and she wears enough makeup for the two of them. Karen scores a couple of caps once in a while and then leaves the bar to chill somewhere, but she doesn't sell heroin and I don't know where she earns her money.

"Haven't seen you in a while," she says.

"Yeah, I've been busy."

"Anything happening?"

I think of telling her that I was out sailing, saw a whale in the bay, and that it had been fucking awesome.

"No," I say. "There'll be some later."

I order a beer for everyone, and shortly after, Deedee brings a guy to our table. They take a seat across from me. He has long, straight hair that come down to the middle of his back and speaks with a forced, effeminate voice.

"I'm Dusty," he says, his hand hanging over the table like the drooping branch of a weeping willow.

I shake hands with him. His fingernails are packed with dirt.

I tell Kangaroo again that I quit using.

"I have people working for me and they're the only ones I deal with," I say with a hint of pride.

"That's good," he says, coming out of his nod, "but you have to watch who you front your stuff to."

Meanwhile, Dusty keeps staring at me, smiling at me without saying a word, and I feel like telling him off, but he's Deedee's friend so I leave it.

The two lesbians are in a party mood. Karen lights up a cigarette and sways to the music in her seat. Captain Kangaroo sits quietly, too busy enjoying the last effects of his fix to speak with anyone. Deedee says something to Dusty and leaves him there while she goes looking. She comes back a few minutes later and deals a couple of caps to Karen. Dusty's filthy hand grabs the glass of beer sitting in front of him and he takes a swig, staring at me over the glass.

The two girls lose interest and stand up.

"We're gonna go party, you want to come with us?" Karen says.

For a moment, I think of taking a break from this scene and go with them to an apartment somewhere in the West End. Just drink and party. No notes and no thinking about the next day. It's enough to see why people go down that road.

"Another time," I say. "I gotta see somebody."

I walk out with them.

"You sure you don't want to come?" Karen asks again once we're outside.

Her girlfriend stands silently, looking at us.

"Thanks, next time."

THE DRUG GAME

Crowley is counting his money, a cigarette hanging from his mouth. He frowns as he rearranges the bills in the stack, placing the faces on the same side like they do at the bank. He's likely going to pick up again.

While Crowley is busy with his bills, Scotty comes over and sits next to him. "You have three?" he asks.

Crowley keeps his eyes down. "I have two left, but it's good."

"Last time it wasn't good." Scotty looks at me to make his point. "I did four and it wasn't even enough."

"This isn't the same stuff!" Crowley argues raising his eyes to look at both Scotty and me. "I did two this morning and it was good enough for me."

"Yeah, okay, sure." Scotty winks at me. "Not like I can go around looking anywhere else."

Crowley spits out the bundle. "It's good, man, I'm telling you."

Scotty pulls out a leather jacket from a bag he's carrying.

"Just bought this leather coat ...beautiful leather," he says.

"Feel how soft it is."

Crowley and I feel the sleeve of the coat.

"It's lambskin."

"Nice," I say.

Scotty smiles again, satisfied. He gives Crowley the money and puts the heroin away. I watch him walk briskly out of the bar, happy.

What a gang, the junkies. They hustle a score by selling dope, or their bodies, or those of their lovers, so they can fix twice a day, and then have some left in the morning to kill the king of hangovers. They eat hardly anything, yet when they do it jams their insides, every part of their bodies taking time off while they nod or wait for the next fix.

They spend the day watching for heat while keeping track of the action better than brokers on the Chicago commodities market. They get the windows of their cars busted by eager cops with baseball bats; they get their teeth broken by a pair of handcuffs and sometimes by the fist of their own supplier. It takes so much work to get in and become a regular addict, that you've got to think that we're doing something right. You've got to think that some of the drug users who come through these doors will say fuck it, too much heat, too much hardship. Maybe even enough hardship to keep some people away from their first heroin high, the one that gets them started. Maybe I, and the cops in uniform, and the Street Crew are doing something right.

I sit back as "Back on the Chain Gang" comes on again over the Blackstone's speakers. On most days, I stretch my beer to one every hour, but tonight I'm drinking too much and I'm beginning to feel my own buzz.

And it's a good buzz.

I look around me. A guy at the centre table gets louder the more he drinks; he makes people laugh, but their laugh is bigger than the jokes. Laughing is what makes them feel good.

The Blackstone is really no different than any other place

where people get together to drink and get high. Drugs or alcohol are part of our lives, and for some, the more there is, the more they use. The junkies and the alcoholics of the Blackstone all have a story. Somewhere in their past, drugs or alcohol fucked them up and put them on this road, but it doesn't matter. The junkies of the Blackstone are constantly chased by the police and they know what they're into. They know what heroin does to them, what they've lost. They've seen friends die and know how easy it is to OD. Yet, they chase it and they'll even help you fix if you ask for it. Help you get into it.

I've had too many drinks, but I enjoy the feeling, especially on a night like this. The music, the sweat, the work I did to get here. Everyone has a story, but I'm not here to hear it, and in any event, they're not keen on sharing it. This isn't the Skids with their down-and-out drug addicts telling their sad stories while sharing a needle in a back alley. Everybody has a connection in the Blackstone and will fight to protect what they have. That's the game they play.

I listen to the music, the weight of the operation sliding off me. I feel the rush and celebrate the fear, the hustle to get here, a new life in a different world. A feeling to remember down the road, when my senses are numbed by desk work. It's all there in front of me, from the first drinks with friends to the row of junkies. It isn't much different than any good party. The chase to get high, the raging good times, and the fall of a sad few while everyone else keeps on going. Like the drummer in a rock band who ends up dying alone in his room, every good party has its victims. Everyone else just keeps on playing.

A HOUSE OF CARDS

"We're shutting down."

We are all sitting around the kitchen table when the team lead-er gets back from the office. Some of the members have their note-books out, making their daily entries.

"We'll give it a couple of weeks, maybe get new faces, and then we wrap it up."

Just like that, it's over.

I get into my car and everything has a different feel. The car is no longer mine, it's a rented police car. My clothes are a disguise. In a few days I'll be gone and all that will be left of my eight months on the street are the tight evidence packages we will take to court in a few months. All I need to do is put my head down and swim hard to the finish line.

I drive down to the Austin and order a beer. Shortly after, Max and Fred walk in and sit with me. They make an odd couple, the old man in his sports jacket and Max in his track suit. Max has a grin on his face.

"We're ready to move again."

Fred listens in, his Ascot cap resting on top of his bald head. He doesn't take anything for granted, taking it one day at a time. He is organized and deliberate, the way a man with over thirty years of jail time ought to be. If he was to be sent back to jail, he once told me, he would prefer to do more than two years so he could be sent to the federal penitentiary, where there is order among the inmates. "In the pen," he said, "you don't have to deal with the nickel-and-dimers who are doing six months for breaking into houses and fighting on the street."

Fred and Max still have access to the same heroin supply, but this is as far as I'll go with them.

"It wasn't great," I complain. "I didn't get as much out of it as I expected."

"You have to add some Epson salt to it," Max says with honest concern, "for the flash.... I got six bundles out of my gram."

"I got sixteen total; I thought I was going to get more."

"I have some put aside for you," Fred says to confirm that he is holding up his end of the deal, "just like we said."

Fred doesn't understand my position. His stuff is good and he knows it.

"I'll get back to you," I say.

It would be better for me to leave, but I sit with Fred and Max, feeling our relationship cool down like a setting sun in winter. A short while later, I'm glad to see Jimmy walk in and stir things up.

"What's happening?" I ask.

"Nothing. Are you in town for a while?"

"Yeah, I'll be around; I have nothing going right now."

"Maybe next time you go to George I'll go with you. Things are quiet here. We can take turns driving, check things out together."

"Not sure when I'm going, but that would be great, man. It's a long drive by myself. It was okay the first time, but now I do it too much. It's a long fucking drive."

Max and Fred listen in, stiff and still.

Nowhere is trust more important than with Jimmy, and he wants to believe that my Prince George story is real. He has put everything on the line, believing in our relationship and what he will get out of it. Max and Fred trusted me because Jimmy has vouched for me. Tiny agreed to talk with me because Jimmy trusted me. Some of the people who sold heroin to me did it because Jimmy said I was good to deal with. He has gambled on me.

A few days later, Max comes to the Austin to see me and I get a sense that things are not going well for him.

"I'm trying to reorganize. I need cash just for a few days ...five hundred. I'll give it back to you with interest."

"Sorry, man, I can't. My cash is all tied up right now."

Turning Max down doesn't sit well with him and I know that it will get back to Jimmy. Everything gets back to Jimmy. And I begin to feel the weight.

Victor walks in with his girlfriend Robin and looks around, his umbrella pinned to the floor. His face lights up when he sees Max and walks straight over.

"I was looking for you," he says to Max, ignoring me.

Victor hangs his umbrella on the chair. It's sunny outside and the umbrella is dry. Max has been spending a lot of time with Victor, putting out a few bundles here and there, and I know that Victor still doesn't trust me. Something doesn't sit well between him and me. We started off on the wrong foot and I never bothered to fix it.

Robin looks at me and says hi. She also dresses well and doesn't look like a hype. The waiter comes and we order beer.

"Can I have a Coke with lots of ice," she asks. "It's crazy hot outside."

Before long, Charlie comes in to score some caps and walks up to our table. Victor steers him to Robin and she sells him six caps.

When Charlie leaves, I tell Robin that I am also looking.

"I don't have anything left with me. Can you wait a few minutes. I'll have to go get it."

"That's okay. I'm in no rush."

"Let me finish my Coke."

Victor grabs her arm.

"Don't sell to him," he says. "You don't even know him."

I'm glad that the others didn't hear him, but I know that the heat is building up, and I don't want to open the lid that holds it down. With traffickers like Victor, heat can sneak up on you and get you hurt before you even see it coming. If I had more time, I would fix it by rebuilding myself. I would get cover story money, the kind that you burn freely with no strings attached, at the right time and in the right places, like a small loan to Max or an expensive dinner with Jimmy and Selina. The kind that makes people believe in you. But my budget doesn't include cover story money and time is running out. I will just have to ride it.

At least I know where I stand with Victor. Unlike Jimmy—and Chico before him—Max and Fred never speak of trust and that worries me.

I leave the Austin knowing that they will talk about me. Telling Fred that I wasn't interested in another deal has changed everything. And turning down Max will hurt me further. I have taken myself out of the group.

COKE FIENDS

I walk out of the Austin and cross Granville toward the Blackstone. A cooler, heavy air has coasted down the stiff peaks of the North Shore, helping me clear my head and get into the right mood. I see Selina standing near her corner down the street. She smiles and gives me a friendly wave as I open the door. The Blackstone isn't full, but many of the regulars are there and I take a seat next to Charlie, near the bar. I feel better. This is my place, and even with all the chaos and the enduring struggles, there is a steadiness to it, like the moving parts of an old diesel engine. The thing about heroin use is that, even if you convince people that you are no longer using, going back to it is the most natural thing. In the Blackstone, no one takes anything for granted and there is honesty to that. I just sit there with Charlie, he and I both quiet and feeling the place. In the Blackstone, you can just sit there and say nothing and it makes sense.

Two uniforms walk in, unhurried, but their eyes scanning the bar.

"I scored some pretty bad stuff yesterday," I say. "Didn't feel a thing, no rush. It was okay, but no rush."

"There's some shit going around," Charlie says, his eyes tracking the cops.

Charlie has skin-popped and he is feeling the gentle buzz.

"How's the stuff you got from Victor?" he asks.

"It's okay."

"At least you got something. People kept coming around looking yesterday and there was nothing."

The cops walk out.

Winding down the operation has taken the pressure off, and I plan to just sit there with the users and catch whatever comes by me. Before long, Captain Kangaroo comes over, and soon after, Deedee walks in accompanied by another trans woman who, like Deedee, is in a jovial mood. The trans woman has just acquired a large hunting knife and is passing it around the table.

Deedee holds it, feeling its weight.

"I like mine better," she says. "This is too big."

Deedee opens her purse and shows me the knife she has inside.

"It's all about show," she says with a smile. "I had this guy turn on me once. I just pulled it out and he calmed right down."

Soon, Scotty comes by, smiling as usual under his thick, dark mop of curly hair and asks if I'm looking. He flops back in a chair and looks around him with interest, not because he's looking for heat, but because he likes the Blackstone crowd. Scotty connects with people. He is gruff-looking, with a permanent five o'clock shadow, but he looks you in the eyes when you speak to him, as if what you have to say matters to him. I want to deal with someone new so I tell him to see me later. He shrugs and walks away.

When Scotty returns, he has a bundle and dishes some of it out to Deedee and the other trans woman who then leave together. He keeps his bundle under the seat next to him.

"Look at that ass," Scotty says looking at the trans woman

walking away. "If you were a girl I'd be all over you!" he yells across the bar. The trans woman turns and smiles.

"Where's Amy?" Scotty asks Charlie.

"I don't know. She's out and about."

Charlie takes a sip of beer, looking straight ahead.

"What do you mean 'she's out and about'?"

"She's a coke fiend."

"She's using coke?" Scotty shakes his head. "Coke's gonna fuck up her head, man."

"I know! No need to tell me. She met this guy, fucking coke-head ...wears nice clothes and everything. Got her doing speed balls and now she's all screwed up.... She's a coke fiend.... I told her to stay away from coke."

"She's finished, man. Don't even try it. Time to move on."

Scotty shakes his head again.

JODIE

"Are you looking?"

"No."

She brings her face close to mine so I can look into her eyes. Her pupils are like two tiny specks of sand on a sea of blue.

"It's good," she says with a smile.

"I can see that," I say, laughing.

Jodie smiles some more, contented.

"That's not Max's stuff, is it?" I ask.

"No, I don't deal with Max anymore."

Cindy comes in alone and asks if I got. It's been a long time since she ripped me off.

"Your old man owes me from the last one," Jodie says to Cindy, lowering her eyelids slowly while her head drifts sideways.

"He's back in the joint," Cindy says matter-of-factly.

The last time I saw Cindy's old man, Spanky, I realized that I didn't need to target him. He couldn't handle the drug and he slowly eroded and melted away like a snowman in spring, a snowman with sunken cheeks and black lines under his eyes. Everyone has a shelf life on the street and his was short. His saving grace is that he was picked up on charges serious enough to send him back to jail where he can clean up, before someone finds him alone and dead in some flophouse with a wet needle sitting on the night table. It's a sad tale anyway you look at it, because I'm sure that someone else had to get hurt for him to be taken away.

"Can I borrow a smoke?" Cindy asks.

Jodie pulls her cigarettes from her purse and gives Cindy a couple. Jodie seems annoyed and should have found a quiet place to enjoy her nod.

"What's he in for?" she asks.

"Got a beef for robbery and one for breach of parole, but I don't care. He'll get cleaned up and he'll be back in a couple of months."

Cindy looks lost without her man. She moves on to another table and tries to get something going with a couple of rounders.

Once Jodie comes out of her nod, we begin to chat about business.

"I like the way you do things," she says studying me. "You're low-key."

"That's the only way."

"We can do good things together," she says with a smile. "I have a good connection."

"Sure," I say, without conviction.

Jodie buys me a beer. She is honest and straight with everyone and I know that she likes me, but I also know the smile. It isn't that of someone who sees herself making money and buying nice things. It's the thought of unlimited supply going into her arm and having a partner to do it with. Unlike Caroline, who likes to say that she "plays" with heroin, Jodie lives it straight on. She's into getting high. But even if she's a wicked drug addict, I like to be with her, take in the honesty and listen to her laugh. On some occasions, I find a sassy spark in her eyes, like that of an outsider looking at the scene from the outside, seeing the lunacy of the place for the first time, and this is when I connect with her. I like her, and she knows it, and I've already gone too far with it. I won't deal with her anymore and I should really push her off. She is already going to jail and there is nothing left for me to do with her, but I like her and let it go on.

Jodie puts her hand on my arm.

"I have to go somewhere. Will you be here when I come back?" she asks.

"Yeah, sure, I'll be here."

Charlie has been listening in on us.

"I thought you were doing something with Max," he says.

"Yeah, but you know Max. He tries to do too much and can't make it happen."

"Yeah I know.... I don't want to deal with him either."

THE END OF MAX

If I have any doubts about Max's fall, Louie Cardinal confirms it when he comes looking for him. Louie is an Indigenous heroin cap dealer who wears a bandana around long black hair that falls straight and shiny down to his lower back. He is quiet, and in this place, the quietness makes him intimidating. He is also smart enough to hire users, who, for a fix, will do the talking and the dealing for him.

Louie comes straight to my table. "Have you seen Max?"

"No ...why? You lookin'?"

"He owes me five hundred bucks for a bundle," he says.

The simple fact that Max is scoring bundles from Louie tells me that he is down and out. In rock climbing, the crux of a climb is the toughest part, where most people fall off. Max climbed to a level where the money was good, but the business harder. He was too cocky and lost his focus. He has fallen off the cliff. Like most drug dealers, the more money Max made, the more chances he took. He took a gamble on me and I'm sure that he has done the same with a number of drug addicts. He got too busy too fast.

Max hasn't done enough jail time, hasn't had the cops break his front door enough, hasn't been ripped off enough by desperate users, or threatened enough by other dealers, to acquire the fear that keeps you out of jail. He got greedy. Drug trafficking is a complicated business. People who have done lots of time don't come out smarter, but they carry a certain amount of fear with them. Not an all-out fear, but the kind that smoulders deep down and makes them look both ways when they leave the house, take that extra turn around the block before getting home, and delay their drug transaction for hours, sometimes days, before they feel comfortable enough to deal. They know the hard side of drug trafficking. They have seen the violence from both the giving and receiving end. They've slept in cramped cells. Max isn't scared enough to last and his street empire is beginning to crumble. The heroin scene is like a sinkhole and anything standing in the same spot for too long will soon or later be swallowed by it. Like me, Max had his run at it and he is now running out of options.

"I haven't seen him," I say.

"Like ...I got the bundle from some pretty heavy people."

I can see fear in the crunched-up lines between Louie's usually steady eyebrows.

"Let's go see if he's at the Austin."

We walk out and I follow Louie across the street. The traffic is dense, and anxious to make his way across, Louie inadvertently blocks the way of a scooter. Its rider yells at him and gives him the finger and Louie walks toward him, erect and serious. The rider steps off his bike, pulls it back to its stand, removes his helmet, and takes on a boxing stance, jumping on his toes. I expect Louie to pull a knife or something, but he stands straight and stiff as the scooter rider throws kicks and punches at him, and soon Louie finds himself sitting on the asphalt, in the middle of Granville Street. The man puts his helmet back on, jumps on his scooter and buzzes away, leaving Louie to gather himself off the pavement. I feel awkward standing by while he gets on his feet. I expected Louie to be a violent man, but he isn't. Like me, he is just putting on a front and it's as if, for a brief moment, he and I understand each other. Silently, we both walk into the Austin where Max sits with Jimmy and Selina. Max's face breaks into a big smile when he sees Louie.

"Hey, man, what's up?"

Louie takes Max aside. He is calm and speaks quietly. Max listens carefully. This time, Louie is in his world, he knows the drug business and it only takes a few words to erase Max's smile.

Louie leaves and Max returns to our table.

"I need to collect five hundred," Max says to Jimmy.

The Man who prided himself on staying clean above the street has now been swallowed by it. Owing money to someone like Louie is never good, so Max has begun to collect from the people who owe him, using Jimmy as his strong arm. Jimmy, the man who embraces the dirty side of crime, with its insane rules, and who sits in the bar getting drunk while his girlfriend works the streets, is now in his element, and I can see it in the implacable look in his face.

"We should be able to get five hundred for Frenchie's stuff," he says, referring to some stereo equipment he had collected from some heroin user who owed Max money.

"I can get you some good stuff," Max says to me, "better than Fred's."

"I'm good for now."

I return to the Blackstone and sit at a table, waiting for something I can latch on. I see young Joe walk in. I haven't seen him since we capped up at his place, and this is good because he hasn't been around for any of my activity since then. He sees me and comes over smiling. He still has the fresh look he had when I first met him, working all night at his house.

"My guy has some good stuff," he says before I can say a word.

"I want to deal directly with him."

I expect some opposition, but Joe sees no problem with me meeting his supplier, and the next day I drive to the Sylvia, a nice hotel on the edge of Stanley Park, away from the Granville action. The man is easygoing, sitting back and relaxed. He has long hair and a Jesus beard and we talk about doing more deals, if I like the product. We do a bundle the easy way—Joe already told me the price and I have the money with me. This could be the beginning of a new job but it will be my last deal with him. Still, the cover team knows him and are happy to get him.

The next day, Max comes down to the Blackstone to see me. He still wants to work with me, but I tell him that I am laying low. I'm guessing that he talked to Joe and knows I just did a deal. He says he still owes the five hundred bucks to Louie Cardinal and needs some money up front to get his business going. He's not happy, but I can take the heat because I know that he will be going to jail in a few days. I just need to watch him until then.

Max leaves and I sit alone until Victor comes down with his girlfriend. I don't know why he comes to the Blackstone—which he almost never does—and chooses to sit with me. He orders some beers and I thank him. After a while, he grabs one of the glasses, and leaning his elbows on the table, takes a sip. He then leans in toward me.

"I can get you anything you want," he says in a cynical tone.

"Good," I say, not wanting to play his game.

"Come on, you never turn down a deal. You're always buying. You want an ounce? ...bundles? ...You want some coke?"

"I'm good."

Victor puts his beer down and leans closer to me, keeping his face into mine.

"Anything you want, I have."

"I'm okay," I say.

Suddenly and violently, Victor throws his fist at my face, stopping it an inch away.

"It would be so easy," he says.

I have my beer glass in my hand and think of smashing it in his face. I get up from my chair.

"See you later, man," I say.

I'm running out of steam. A few hours later Jimmy and I get together. There is still a strong bond between us, the kind that could not break the easy way, and with only a few days left before the roundup, I need to maintain that bond. So we have some beers and I speak again about the score in Prince George. I tell him that I am still waiting for a specific person to go away on vacation before we can have access to the money.

"I have to be careful in Prince George," I say. "The bulls have been giving me heat. The tricky part will be to bring the money down to Vancouver." ·

Jimmy's eyes sparkle. It isn't the greed, but the thought that something will soon happen to confirm that he and I are good, and that he did right when he introduced me to Max. He is looking for a good ending to this story.

"Max's wife and Selina can go over there," he says, "and bring the money back. Nobody knows them over there and two women won't bring too much attention to themselves."

I'm surprised to hear Jimmy bring Max into this deal. It tells me that he is also using it to keep Max on side.

"That's good. You need to see Tiny?"

"Yeah, as soon as Selina gets back."

"I'll go with you ...we'll take my car."

"I gotta find Selina first."

Jimmy walks out of the bar a couple of times looking for her. I stay out of it.

When they return together, Selina rummages through her purse and pulls a roll of bills, which she gives to Jimmy. He counts the bills and looks at her.

"After all that time?" he asks.

"I could've had one early, but the cops came by."

She sits next to him.

"I have to do a run. I'll see you at the house," Jimmy says.

"Hurry," Selina says with impatience.

He gives her a kiss and looks at me with a smile.

"My little Fiji girl." He caresses the back of her neck with his hand.

Jimmy and I walk to my car and we drive to Tiny's bar. I'm hoping to give him one more try.

Tiny is in a bad mood, but he gives Jimmy what he wants. Jimmy stuffs the plastic bag in the breast pocket of his leather coat. Getting caught with pills isn't a big concern for him. Pills don't bring on jail time.

"Anything around?" Jimmy asks.

"Yeah. There's a lot of heat around. You have to watch who you deal with."

Tiny looks at me in a way that makes me wonder if I am getting paranoid.

"There's morphine around," he continues.

"No H?" I ask.

"Morphine's a lot cleaner than heroin. Ask Jimmy."

"Yeah, but it has to be good," Jimmy clarifies.

"They have to add all sorts of chemicals to the morphine to make heroin," Tiny explains. "Morphine's a lot cleaner."

"When can you do it?" I ask.

"Talk to Jimmy in a couple of days."

"How much for a quarter."

"Forty-five ...talk to Jimmy."

"I need it before Friday. Can you do it?"

"Talk to Jimmy."

Jimmy and I start for the door when Tiny calls for Jimmy.

Jimmy goes back to the bar and Tiny gives him a good serious talk. Jimmy keeps saying "yeah, yeah no problem," and seeing Tiny glance at me, I know that I've pushed too hard to get Jimmy out of the way.

On the way back, Jimmy doesn't talk much.

"Let me deal with Tiny," he says after a while.

"Sure."

The traffic is heavy and it makes the air in the car even heavier.

After we arrive at the Blackstone, we meet with Selina. I score a cap from Captain Kangaroo and the three of us walk to Jimmy and Selina's place on Davie Street. They are getting ready to move to North Vancouver and boxes are stacked in the kitchen. Jimmy and Selina face each other at the small table with the pretty flowers on the windowsill. I sit at the end of the table.

Jimmy uses a spoon to crush the pills into a fine dust. Selina goes to a kitchen drawer and comes back with another spoon. They don't speak, as if they were making coffee together. The spoon is crooked, it has been bent a few times and the bottom is charred. She put some water in it and gives it to me so I can fix my cap of heroin. I do what I am trained to do, ensuring that no heroin enters my body. Next to me, Jimmy is already pulling his cloudy broth of crushed tablets into the syringe. He picks up Selina's hand and turns it around gently to find a good vein. He frowns and she looks with interest at the needle sliding into her flesh. I feel like I am part of something private and should not be here, but they aren't looking at me. She mixes another spoonful, and knowing his good veins, swiftly slides the needle into Jimmy's wrist.

After we fixed, Jimmy is more relaxed about me. Even seems happy. We let some time pass by.

"When do you want to go to Prince George?" Jimmy asks later on.

"Let's do it next Thursday. I have to do the job on a Friday. The girls can be back by Monday."

He is eager to get it done and keeps on working out scenarios.

"The girls can go the day before and we can follow in a separate car on Thursday," he says. "We'll have to stash the money for a while after we get back."

We walk across the street and order some beer. Jimmy and Selina aren't wasted. They never are. But Jimmy gets anxious about the deal.

"It's got to happen next week," he says.

"It's done, man," I say, touching his glass with mine.

This gives me time to work a deal with Caroline's connection, Lenny. He's an old-timer with a lot of history and my office wants to get him.

We go to the Austin. Caroline comes to see me and I am beginning to recognize the user in her. I see it in the lines under her eyes and in the way she walks. Gone is the spark she had the first day I saw her. Gone are the looks and smarts that used to light up the room around her, the very thing, ironically, that helped her make connections and access good supplies of heroin. Heroin is taking its toll; even the colour of her skin has turned from gold to ash.

Victor and Max also come and sit at our table, but they don't talk to me. Jimmy turns to them as if I weren't there and talks about collecting money again, this time for Victor. I'm an outsider again. I was always an outsider. They stop talking as Caroline and I get up and walk away. I can feel their eyes on me.

ANOTHER DEAL WITH CAROLINE

"Lenny's ready to deal," Caroline says, "but he doesn't want to meet anybody."

"Is it good?"

"Eight to one …the best around. You can ask Charlie."

"I don't want to screw around."

"You won't. Trust me."

"Do you trust him?"

"Yes, he's good."

"I want to meet him."

"I'll ask, but he already told me he doesn't want to meet any-body."

She looks at my hair.

"You need a haircut. We can talk upstairs."

We take the elevator to the third floor. Once in her room, I take a seat on a chair, facing a small table and a mirror against the wall. Hairbrushes, combs, scissors, and clippers sit on the table. As she cuts my hair, I look through the mirror at the room behind her. Like most hotel rooms built in the early 1900s, it is small but solid, with intricate trim and ceiling details covered with numerous thick coats of creamy paint. A small window overlooks Granville Street. The room is clean, but the furniture and bed are plain and the walls are bare. I think of her alone in the room, "playing" with heroin. On the bed, a blue dress gives the room a splash of colour. I have seen this dress on her before, at a time when her face was still full, her eyes bright, and she had looked good and smart in it.

"He wants $4,500 for a quarter," Caroline says, "the same as before."

"It's a lot of money."

"If you want a good price, we need to go to Toronto," she says as she has done before, "but for here it's a good deal. If you want it, I'll go see him now."

Once my hair is cut we walk down and cross Davie to the Theodore where Caroline buys a pack of cigarettes.

"Where are we going?" I ask.

"The Georgia."

We drive to the Georgia Hotel and Caroline goes inside to look for the man. She comes back a few minutes later.

"He's not here, but there's a girl waiting for him. She said he never showed up."

I'm not too worried. Anything can stop a deal in its track: a car that follows you more than a couple of blocks; a "click" heard on the telephone, which really has nothing to do with any wiretaps; anything that doesn't fit. For all I know, her supplier could have been watching us come in just to see if I brought the heat. I don't blame him, Caroline is too anxious to get this deal going and she isn't careful. We return to the Austin, and as I round the corner of Davie and Granville Street, Caroline perks up.

"There he is!"

A man in his forties, neatly dressed in a short brown leather jacket with an open collar shirt and dark slacks, stands at the pay phone at the entrance of the Austin. I know this is Lenny because I saw his picture at the Shack. He is a well-connected Hungarian dealer with a long criminal record. He also looks like the man I saw checking for heat in New Westminster. He is looking at us as I pulled over and Caroline goes to him.

He listens to Caroline, but keeps his eyes on me. Caroline seems to get increasingly animated. After a while, he walks away and turns his head enough to take another look at me. Caroline returns to my car.

"He's freaking out because someone told him that I took you to his place. He wants to talk to Charlie in about an hour."

I park my car behind Theo's and Caroline and I walk to the lounge at the Austin. We wait a half hour for Charlie to come, but he doesn't show, so we go looking for him in the Blackstone. He isn't there, so Caroline gets all hyper and I follow her back to the Austin, where she goes to the front desk to get Charlie's room number. Caroline calls him from the lobby, and a few minutes later, Charlie comes down to meet us. He is unshaven, wearing a heavy terry-cloth robe and a pair of leather slippers. His face is long, drawn, and the ends of his moustache droop down below his chin, making his morose face even longer.

"Lenny wants to speak with you," Caroline says. "I need you to fix this deal."

Charlie shrugs. Caroline dials the number and Charlie takes the receiver. He throws a few glances at both Caroline and me while listening on the receiver.

"He wants us to meet him in New West," Charlie says after hanging up, "at three."

I look at my watch. We have about forty-five minutes.

"I have to put some shoes on," Charlie says looking down at his slippers.

Caroline and I walk out to get the car and wait for Charlie in front of the Austin. Caroline raises the back of her hand to her forehead.

"I can't believe it," she says. "What a mess."

Charlie comes down and we drive to New Westminster.

Caroline turns to Charlie. "Is he upset?"

"I don't know. He's always cagey."

We arrive at a gas station and sit in the lot until a brown Mercury Cougar drives up to the pumps. Lenny steps out and fills the tank.

"There he is," says Charlie as he opens the door.

Caroline watches Charlie walk to the 7-Eleven.

"Give me the money ...quick!" she says to me.

I count out the $4,500 and give it to her. She pulls up her dress, and as if she was acting out a role in a TV show, slips the roll into the top end of her stocking.

"How much is Max getting out of this?" Caroline asks.

"Nothing," I answer.

"I can't believe it! He was supposed to give me a piece of it."

"He has nothing to do with this. It's all mine."

"Charlie and I were going to score a bundle for ourselves, but I don't know if he has enough money. At least, can I get a hit after the deal?"

"No."

"No?"

She looks at me with surprise.

"I took a chance on you," she says, crossing her arms and looking ahead.

"I know, but I have to leave right away."

"I just want a crack at it, just one hit."

I shake my head.

"I can't believe it. What a mess. Max led me to believe that a part of it was his. I worked for two days on this."

"Max's got nothing to do with it."

"I'm very tired, and now I have to give two-fifty to Charlie. Half of my commission, and I have nothing to show for it."

She crosses her arms, shakes her head.

"I want a piece of it," she says again. "I'll pay you," she pleads.

"I can't. A piece of it here means a lot of profit down the line and I just want to get out of here."

"Any amount?"

"No, I can't do it. These things are complicated. They don't always turn out the way you want."

"This was a mistake," she says again.

Charlie comes to the car window. He looks at me.

"Give me the money."

Caroline steps out of the car, digs under her dress and retrieves the $4,500 I gave her. She gives the money to Charlie, no longer caring about the formalities of drug trafficking. She slumps back into her seat.

"I knew I shouldn't have gotten involved."

"I just want to get out of here," I say. "We'll talk later. These deals always get screwed up one way or another."

After giving Lenny the money, Charlie comes back and sits in the back of the car.

"Let's get out of here," he growls.

We drive back silently. Charlie pulls out a plastic baggie wrapped in scotch tape out of his pants and passes it to me. I feel Caroline's stare burn my hand as I reach down to tuck the package into my sock. We drive back to the Austin, Caroline staring ahead, dejected. Charlie just wants to get back to his bed.

SPAGHETTI DINNER

There are only a couple of days left before we wrap up the operation. The cover team and I are having our monthly spaghetti dinner. We've been doing this with the coke team for a few months now. They arrive early and are having a heated discussion; their agent doesn't like the way the operation is going and wants more money. Working with an agent brings along a different set of problems. Unlike informants, who merely provide information, agents are involved in the deals and make drug purchases for evidence. They need training and supervision.

"We've been pushing him hard. He's just feeling the heat," says the team leader.

"I know he's gonna be a good witness. Have you seen his notes? They're better than mine," says the agent's handler.

"He's got a good contract," says the team leader. "Plus he'll be taken care of after the operation. In my days, all they got was some cash and a plane ticket out of town."

For their part, the two undercover operators like working

with the agent. This is good because some agents can be difficult. I worked with agents before and there's nothing like a good professional agent to get you to a target, even if a bad one can be deadly. A good agent can save you months of surveillance and futile wiretap interceptions. Members of criminal organizations know this too well, and the coke team's agent will have to leave town after the operation. However you look at it, it takes guts to do what they do.

We settle around the dinner table. Heaping plates of spaghetti steaming under a thick meat sauce sit on the table. It's good to take a day off together and put the drug business aside to chat about other things over a dinner and a bottle of wine. Just a group of men and women doing the same job, talking about the things they have in common: who's getting promoted, the new car someone just bought, music, and sports. Nothing about the people we meet in the Blackstone or in the coke bars. They stop existing when we're done with our operational meetings. Undercover operators get to live a different life for a while, but it isn't theirs. Whether they need to show up for a meeting at an expensive restaurant in LA, or have to work in a factory during the day so that they can live the life of a speed addict at night, the job is the same.

As intense as everyone is during the job, it's still a job. A job we all love because there is no other like it and because it is a job that cannot be done without passion. It takes us to the action as it happens and feeds adrenalin through our veins whenever fear tightens up our belly. Days are never the same and the unexpected is expected. Undercover operators can develop many relationships during an operation and sometimes the connection is real. There are people we get along with, and people we despise. Some, we fear. But we never take these relationships outside of the operation. We would never have met our targets if we weren't cops and the person they know in us ceases to exist the day of the roundup. I guess it's just like any other police work. We feel sadness for some and anger towards others, but we keep it to ourselves because, before anything else, we are the eyes and ears of the justice system, getting the evidence and taking notes on what goes on so we can bring it to court. That's the game we all play, in uniform or sitting in a bar with needle tracks in our arms.

In a few days, everything will be over, but a side of me wants to keep going, like a fisherman out on the water at dusk, waiting for one more bite. This chase, going from one buy to another, and the adrenaline I get from just walking into the bar and taking on whatever comes, has kept me going for eight months now and I don't have anything to replace it. It has become the reason why I get up in the morning. For the cover team, the drive to get buys and put drug traffickers in jail is also there. They worked with me on every deal, standing by, doing checks, working on the leads we have, and trying to watch over me. But under all of this, everyone is tired. In a couple of days it will be over. We'll turn the page and move on.

FULL CIRCLE

The cover team members decide to work on Lenny and see if he'll do a deal directly with me. Like Max, George, and Serge the vicious weed dealer, Lenny is into it for the money, and as long as people are addicted to something, there'll be people like him to give them what they want and more. Lenny is part of an Eastern European connection. He has been to jail, but he keeps going and his name keeps surfacing in informant debriefings. Everyone will be happy if I can arrange something for the wrap-up, hoping that we can take him down dirty.

I take a walk to the Austin lounge and see Caroline sitting with an elderly Chinese man.

"How's it going?" I ask as I walk by.

"Okay," she says. "If you want Dilaudids, I have some."

"How much?"

"Fifty."

To most addicts, Dilaudid is a good clean high. The man looks purposely away, and I have no doubts that she is selling the pills for him. Given Chinese organized crime connections with Asian supplies of heroin, I would normally try to get closer to him, but I'm not interested in pills so I walk away to the bar area. When I glance back, Caroline and her man are already gone. Of all the addicts I met during the operation, she is the one who was changed the most from heroin. Steady users like Charlie, Jodie, and Captain Kangaroo have remained the same since the first time I saw them. It's as if they found a way to live with the heroin. I'm sure that they've hurt plenty of people close to them on their way to addiction, burning bridges with friends and family until there is no one left, but they have settled into their own ways. They are alone now, even when they hang around together, each driven by the thought of a good high, or the fear of a harsh sickness. Only Deedee seems to make a go of it, all flutter and smiles, as if heroin was an afterthought. She is kind and likes people, and more than anyone, seems to understand the place.

I walk back to the Blackstone and see Jodie sitting with Charlie.

"There's nothing around," Charlie says.

I scan the bar around me. Far on the other side, Palmer sits at his regular table near the bar, his eyes scanning the place under his cowboy hat. As for Cindy, her old man is back in the joint pumping iron and getting his wasted body back to shape. I can expect them to be together again in a few months. A few of the faces I grew accustomed to are now gone and a few new ones are emerging to the scene. Some are in jail and some have returned from it; some have overdosed. I could be starting another operation and nothing would be different. I've come around full circle.

Kitty comes down to our table and I buy a round of beer.

"The problem with this place is that you can't get anything going steady," I say.

"I'm doing okay," Jodie says.

"How do you do it?"

"I know people and I'm not greedy."

"That's true. You're not greedy," Kitty says. "My old man was greedy and he's in the joint. He was trying to do too many deals. Can't do too many deals without the bulls knowing about it ...I told him ...can't do that many deals."

As if Kitty's rant had called them in, two uniformed cops enter. Charlie and Kitty are sitting with their backs against the wall. Their eyes follow the cops making their way around the bar.

"You haven't been around for a while," I say to Jodie.

"I went to see my sister in the Interior."

"Where?"

"Penticton."

"Never been there."

"If you come, I'll show you around."

"Yeah, we should go someday."

Jodie smiles.

I have known Jodie for about six months and I could not find anything bad to say about her.

"What's in Penticton?" I ask.

"A lake ...orchards everywhere. It's good. I know a lot of people there. I have family there."

"Sounds awesome."

"We could do business there."

I don't know what would happen if I were an addict and got together with Jodie. I only know that, before Jodie and I could get together and drive to some town away from Vancouver, heroin would have to be sorted out. Going to Penticton would get us away from Vancouver's heroin scene, but it doesn't matter. Everywhere you go there's somebody like Max with a supply of high-grade heroin or a Ziploc baggie full of Percocet, Oxycodone, or Dilaudid. Some are coming out with freebase heroin so that it can bypass the bloodstream and go straight to your brain. I've seen the complicity of two addicts who turn into lovers. Sometimes, the relationship will implode in an orgy of drugs, but I've also seen it work itself out into a steady life organized around daily fixes. Some old-timers do it, some of them often talking to the police to protect the nest. Jodie is a nice girl and if she didn't use, we'd get along on pretty well anything. I don't know what makes us different, why she is a user and I'm not.

We drink beer and laugh. Jodie doesn't speak anymore about Penticton, but we're getting close to a heroin relationship.

"We should work together," she says.

I smile.

"We really should," she insists.

I know that, in a couple of days, it will be over, and that we will never work together. She will hate me for letting her know that I like her. The heroin addict in her is right. There is no need to get into anything else until the heroin is sorted out.

GETTING BACK AT JIMMY

Jimmy walks in the Austin and pulls out a chair at my table without saying a word.

"What's happening?" I ask.

"Nothing's happening. You had something good with Max and you let it go."

"I know I fucked up. We'll do things again me and him."

"You still ready for Thursday," he asks.

"Yeah, yeah, we're still on. Have you heard from Tiny?"

"I'm still waiting."

"Is he there?"

"Yeah, he's there. We can go later, but I'm not sure he wants to deal with you."

Tiny's suspicion sits on the table like a spill of stale beer.

"We found a place in North Van," he says after a while.

"That's great," I say as I get up. "Are you still gonna be around later?"

"Yeah, Selina and I will come down."

I leave Jimmy sitting there by himself and walk over to the Blackstone. Before long, the sidewalk bikers come in with their girls and sit next to me. We've been getting along in the past weeks, but their business is coke and marijuana and I never talk drugs with them.

The bikers talk about the heat and they say that, earlier in the day, they had a run-in with the "pigs" at Theo's. They're in a good mood and we move a few tables together so more people can join in. Before long, the tables are covered with glasses of beer, and I soon find myself in the kind of groove where a couple of hours can pass you by in the blink of an eye.

A short while later, Charlie walks in and stands a few tables over, looking at me. He nods and I follow him to a table along the wall.

"If you're looking, Amy can help you out. It's very good. She has coke too," he says, "but she doesn't touch the coke," he adds quickly. "I told her, 'you do coke and it's over.'"

"How much for the horse?"

"Five thousand a street ounce. That's a forty-gram ounce."

"When can she do it?" I ask.

"A couple of days."

"Yeah, okay. I want an ounce. The earlier the better," I say, knowing that the odds of putting this together before the roundup are close to nil.

As I walk back to my seat, I cross paths with Jimmy, who has just arrived. He brings his head close to mine and mumbles something.

"What?" I ask.

He is both drunk and on the nod, and I can't understand what he says. He brings his face closer and opens his mouth. I see a balloon tied with a knot back in his throat. It's the first time I see Jimmy deal; first time I see him fucked-up by drugs. I look at him and feel a mix of pity and disgust.

"No, thanks ...I'm not looking."

I sit at my table and look around me. The Blackstone appears to me like the sad place that it is. It's Welfare Wednesday, like the first night I spent here, but there is no challenge left, no one to work up to. Scotty is playing pool and Captain Kangaroo is sitting in his usual chair. To think of it, I haven't seen Crowley for a while so I figure that he has gone to jail. But heroin will still be coming tonight, tomorrow, and the next day. Hypes will go to jail and hypes will die. Some will end up on the Skids of Hastings Street, along with other drug and alcohol abusers, and the mentally ill. I thought of all the time spent on the Granville Strip with Jimmy, telling stories and looking for action together. I think of the time he got Serge to hit Melanie one more time. I think of his moronic code of the streets, upheld by violence and stupidity, of Selina, and all the times Jimmy and I sat over a beer while she stood alone on her street corner. I like him and we're friends and it's fucking me up. I look at him sitting there, out of it and alone, with a bundle in his mouth, and I do something I never did before in the middle of an operation. I walk to the pay phone and call the cover team. I return to my seat with the bikers and order a round.

They come with quickness in their steps and from all directions until a hand grabs Jimmy's throat and someone punches him in the stomach, and as quick as it started, one of the cops has the bundle in his hand. Jimmy sits there, his eyes crossed, his cheeks swollen as if he was going to throw up, and his body swaying like a dry reed on a windy fall day.

The biker next to me is angry. He looks at me and makes his hand flutter rapidly over his heart, letting me know that adrenaline, likely with the help of coke or speed, is making his heart beat fast. I shake my head but I don't feel the adrenaline. We watch the police put Jimmy on his feet and walk him out, his hands behind his back. I can't say it feels good, watching him walk out surrounded by cops, but it brings me back to where I belong. This is his world and I am leaving it. Still, I don't like to think of Jimmy going sick on that jail cot.

"Fucking pigs," the biker says to me.

We drink some more.

I DON'T LIKE THIS PLACE

The next day, I meet Charlie sitting at a table in the Austin.

"Can Amy still do it?" I ask.

"Haven't seen her. We broke up."

"You gotta let go of that roller coaster. Man, she's gonna fuck you up."

We watch the scene before us. The bar is full and the strippers busy.

"I saw Lenny last night," Charlie continues. "He's still asking about you. I told him you're okay."

"Does he still want to do business?" I ask.

"Why do you think he was asking?"

"Tell him I'm interested. But I want to deal directly with him."

"You gonna cut me out, aren't you."

"The cops are all over you."

Charlie smiles, "I know I'm a heat bag."

I walk over to the Blackstone and am surprised to see Lenny sitting there with a tall and bulky Indigenous guy. I take a chair next to him, and since we were never introduced to each other, he looks ahead without paying attention to me. He is the Man and I haven't earned the right to deal directly with him. The bulky guy stares directly at me, serious.

"What's happening?" I ask.

"Not much," Lenny says.

"Listen, we need to work things out," I press on.

Lenny keeps his eyes looking straight ahead, his hired muscle keeps his eyes on me.

"I didn't like the way it went last time," I continue.

Lenny lights up a cigarette. His bulky companion stares at me and leans in.

"I don't want to talk about it," Lenny says.

"Next time we should do it just you and me."

"I don't want to talk about it."

The Indigenous man turns his chair slightly towards me. His hands on his thighs and his right leg jumping up and down. He keeps on staring at me, looking for me, and I need to watch him. I try to ignore him, but I know that he will find me one way or another if I stay long enough.

"Is there anything around?" I ask.

"Yeah, but it's not very good. The thing to do is to go to Amsterdam. I know people there."

"Can't be easy to arrange something over there."

"I know people there."

Any heroin user who goes to Amsterdam can find his way to score. Lenny just wants my money so he can turn himself into an importer. Even if I had the time, there wouldn't be a deal with Lenny. I am only interested in established networks that already bring heroin to the streets of Vancouver, not in building an importation network.

Lenny and I look at the people all around us, neither of us belongs here. Heroin users have nothing to do with the game we play, he for the money, and I for the law. If I weren't too tired to get something going with him, I'm sure I could come up with something, put on a new face and act like a high roller. I do it in other operations, where an informant has already put in the time before I show up nice and fresh for the introduction. But after several months sitting here in the Blackstone, it's like I've become part of it and can't find the words that will get me out. Maybe something like telling him that he shouldn't deal with Caroline, that she's green and will burn him just from being careless. That I don't want to deal with her. But the words don't come to me and I'm stuck. It's like I made it to the edge of town, but still can't get out, feeling everything I know and work for pulling me back. Lenny operates in a different world. He deals in heroin so he can pay for his expensive apartment, his nice clothes, and his own fix. He never comes to the Blackstone, and I have nothing left to take myself out of it.

"I don't like this place," I say. "Do you like this place?"

"I don't like this place."

Lenny picks up his cigarette pack and leaves, taking his hired hand with him, along with any chance I have to deal with him.

Now that dealing with Lenny is out, I need to concentrate on finishing this job. I wonder if anyone is aware that Jimmy has been jumped, but I don't want to bring it up. Calling the Street Crew on him was a bad move, especially when I was the last person to know that he had been holding heroin before he was jumped. It doesn't help that I am already losing the trust of just about anyone who has already dealt with me, but with only a couple of days left, there is no need to try to patch things up. I'll just keep my head straight and deal with anyone who still trusts me.

Victor comes over and sits with me. I figure that he knows about Jimmy.

"The cops came by yesterday and checked me out. The one cop, he said, 'so, you're the famous Victor Szabo.' Hear that? I am fucking famous," he says. "Fucking famous!"

I pick up my glass and drink the beer. Victor looks at me.

"What about you. Are you famous with the cops?" he asks, looking at me square. I stare back at him, drink some more of the beer, and think, for the second time, of smashing my glass into his face.

PLAYING THE GAME

It's my last day and I'm trying to save whatever is left of my under-cover life to drum up one more deal. I step out of my car and walk directly to the Austin, where I find Caroline chatting with Charlie over a beer.

"What's happening with Lenny?" I ask.

"He's pissed because you don't want to deal through me," Charlie says.

"Nothing to do with you, man."

"I know, I know how it is, but that's the way he is."

"We can't work something out, Lenny and me, if we don't talk."

A while later, two uniformed cops come in. They are new to the scene, letting us know that they have arrived, a young, female cop in a ponytail and a bodybuilder's build with a young man who wears a broad smile. I catch the blue of their pants near our table and it makes me nervous.

"You got ID?" the woman asks.

They take our names down and do their radio checks.

After they have gone, the waiter comes to see us.

"If you guys are gonna bring the heat here, you gonna have to go," he says.

Charlie stands up. "I'm the heat bag," he says to the waiter before leaving.

With Charlie gone, Caroline sits next to me.

"I need to talk to you?" she says, her smooth, skinny arms resting on the table. "Not here, let's go and talk somewhere."

We walk to my car and drive along a crowded Davie Street. Caroline lights a cigarette.

"People are talking about you."

Stopping at Burrard, I watch the people cross the street in front of us. Couples with and without children enjoying the night.

"What are they saying?"

"They say you're a cop."

"I really don't care," I say as my car speeds up along Davie. "I've heard it before. I'm just careful and it rubs people the wrong way."

Caroline is not listening to what I have to say.

"If you're a cop, you're good," she says, probing me with her eyes.

I know that Caroline is playing me, but for a fraction of a second, I wonder if I could get her to work with us. She could turn me to some good targets, the ones that make the money. After all, that's what this little drive is about. I feel the complicity and I know that she feels it too. Something in me wants to talk straight with her, leave all the lies and games behind. That complicity was there from the time I met her, and it it's still there now that she's looking for a way out. She would be a great agent if she stopped using, but my job is to stay in my role and leave it to the cover team to talk to her.

"They can say what they want, but that kind of talk is what's fucking me up," I say, meeting her gaze.

"I don't think you're a cop," she says smiling, her eyes still locked on me, both of us playing the game.

We drive down to Denman, where the green, lush vegetation of Stanley Park meets the buildings of the West End. Out on the calm, blue water, foreign ships anchored in the bay wait patiently for their turn to come in.

"I called my people in Toronto," Caroline says.

"What did they say?"

"We can go anytime."

I drop Caroline off at the Austin and walk alone to the Blackstone. Tomorrow, the drug teams will pick her up along with the others and it will be over. They will be brought into the lock-up, one by one, and I will meet them for the first and last time as a police officer. For most, it will be all business. People like Crowley, Frank, and Charlie knew they were taking a chance with me and they never invested much emotion into it. With some there will be hatred. At the end, it all started with heroin and the addicts will do what they do, some striking a deal, some going to jail. To the other officers, they will be drug traffickers caught in their own game. I won't feel the same about some of them. Addiction changes everything.

One after the other, they will stand on the same spot, but their story couldn't be more different. Jimmy will look at me, beating himself up for vouching for me. He will have to leave town. Deedee will laugh it off; heroin and the law are only a sidebar to her life. With Jodie, the friendship is important and it will hurt her, but it will only take her a few minutes of anger to rid herself of any human connection that may have existed.

The cops around me will be glad to see Max, and then Fred, stand next to me. Sometimes, it isn't only about the drug. I once bought a bag of weed in a small town from a guy who was a prime suspect in a case where a girl was left for dead in the woods after being raped and beaten up. He was the town bully and had also threatened to kill a policeman. We met in the washroom and he did the deal the easy way. I wasn't there when he was arrested, but

I'm sure that it felt good to the local cops. I never saw him in court because he committed suicide before the trial. There is always a story.

Everyone I'll meet on the roundup will be different, but I won't be judging them. I got too close to Jimmy and got angry, but I have to leave it all behind. Some came to the Blackstone for the crime, some for the drugs. Jimmy and I got along because he's a street criminal first, always looking for a score. For some of the others, it's about the drug and not being alone. There's a world of difference between the two, but to the court and in my job, it's all the same.

LEAVING TOWN

I could shut it down, but chose to sit alone against the wall when Jimmy and Selina come in to see me. Jimmy has been released from jail and a court date has been set. He isn't allowed on the Granville Strip, but it's still early afternoon and the cops haven't begun their regular walks.

"Anything happening?" he asks.

"I gotta meet somebody in about an hour," I say. "He owes me money."

I look at Selina.

"How's the new place?"

"Great."

She gives Jimmy a kiss and walks away to her street corner.

"You gonna be around?" Jimmy asks.

"Sure."

Jimmy didn't bring up his arrest and I can't tell whether he feels that I had anything to do with it. I finish my beer and walk across the street to the Austin. It is early and the sun is high and bright.

Before entering, I look down Granville Street and see Selina standing alone on the sidewalk.

The Austin is quiet and Caroline is gone. I feel an emptiness inside, already realizing that I don't belong. I walk out and cross the street again. Selina is no longer standing on her corner. I pull on the heavy door and let my eyes adjust to the Blackstone's dimmed emptiness. Looking at the tables against the wall I am glad to find Captain Kangaroo sitting at his usual table.

"Anything happening?" I ask, taking a seat next to him.

"Just got here. What's going on with you?"

"Not much. I'm waiting for a score, but I don't think its gonna happen."

"It's good to let things cool down sometimes."

Deedee comes in and sits across from us. She opens her purse and looks frantically through it.

"What the fuck!" she cries out.

She finally smiles and brings out a roll of bills, pulls a few out and gives a sign to the waiter. She goes back into her purse and fixes her makeup.

"Where are you from, Deedee?"

"I'm from Saint Catharines, in Ontario."

"Do you miss it?"

"I miss my family, but my brother is here so that helps. I like it here, there's no better place in the world. Why do you ask?"

"Nothing, I'm thinking of moving back."

"Don't do it. Just give it time. I used to feel the same way, but you got to give it time. People are good here."

Jimmy comes in and stands by the door. He gives me a nod and I walk up to him. This time, he is upbeat and tells me that Tiny is still interested in dealing with me. I have nothing else going so I figure that one more trip to Tiny's bar can't hurt.

"Sure, sounds good."

We cross Granville Street and walk through Theo's where the

waiter leans his back against the bar.

"Hey Nick, how's it going? You gonna have a beer?"

"No thanks. We have some errands to do. Maybe later."

Jimmy walks to a table and talks to two guys I haven't seen before.

"What's Jimmy got you into now?" he jokes.

"You know how it is," I say as Jimmy walks back with the two guys.

"Tiny isn't around, so let's go to my house in North Van," he says. "These guys are coming with us."

The four of us walk out to the back parking lot and get into my car. It's a nice clear afternoon as we cross the Lions Gate Bridge and the sun splashes spears of silver all the way to the Pacific. The mountains loom ahead of us, already taking on a shade of purple.

"Must be good to live on the North Shore," I say.

"Yeah. It's nice and quiet."

I look at Jimmy and it feels strange to be driving in the suburbs with him and his friends. The car is silent and I keep turning scenarios over in my head. None seems to work.

When we arrive at Jimmy's house, the two men stand in the driveway.

"Great place," I say to Jimmy.

"Yeah, business is good."

We all start for the house, the two guys walking ahead of Jimmy and me. I hold back but Jimmy stays close to me.

"Let's have a beer or something," Jimmy says as he enters. I follow him and stop inside the entrance hallway. The two men have already gone into the living room. They both stand and look at us. I let the screen door close slowly behind me so the latch won't catch. I look at Jimmy and smile.

"Listen, I'm gonna have some money together tonight. You gonna be at the Austin later on?"

"Yeah, sure, let's go inside and sit down."

"No thanks, I just remembered I gotta meet Chico in town ...totally forgot...."

I glanced at the two men still standing in the living room. One of them is reading a newspaper he has picked up from the coffee table.

"...plus you got things to do, so let's get together tonight and talk about it."

I take a step back across the doorsill, holding the screen door open.

"We need to talk about that other thing. I'm ready to go to George. Can even go tomorrow. Could you and Selina go tomorrow if you had to?"

"No, I can't tomorrow."

"Talk to Selina about it. It'll be good," I say still smiling. "Let's make it happen, Jimmy, the Austin at ten."

I walk back to my car and Jimmy comes out to watch me back onto the street. He stands alone on the porch, following me with his eyes, his face devoid of expression, Jimmy the user and street player, the pimp, my friend, standing straight and unyielding.

I drive off and don't look back.

Crossing the Lions Gate Bridge I look at the city ahead of me with its great buildings surrounded by blue water and green mountains. I continue on to the shadows of the Granville Street hotels. It's late afternoon and I know that the junkies are now on the move looking to score. A girl pulls on the heavy door of the Blackstone and disappears inside. The place is filling and the junkies are waiting, but, this time, I will not be stopping. Instead, I will drive by, and like the others around me, will not see them.

I take my leather jacket off for the last time. The lining is discoloured and smells of sweat. I'll remember to throw it out when I get home.

EPILOGUE

A month following the operation, I was posted to the heroin unit target team. My time was shared between drug investigations and appearing in court, where I saw the people I met in the Blackstone for the first time since the roundup. They looked at me silently while I pulled out my notes and told the story. Some were fined and others were sent to jail. I don't know where they are now.

The heroin target team worked higher-level targets, but like any drug team, our team needed informants, and on a quiet day, we would sit on a dealer and wait for someone we knew to show up. On one of those days, an old, beat-up car showed up at the house we were watching. A man in his forties, scrawny and hunched over, walked out of the house after a few minutes and drove away. We took it down a few blocks away, squeezing his car into the traffic and running to the driver's door to prevent him from swallowing the drugs. He stood on the sidewalk while I searched his car for the second time.

I pulled the cover of the gearshift and found the drug, a few caps in a plastic bag, and called "bingo," showing the bag to the other investigator. And then I looked at the man. There was no expression in his face, but I could read the resignation in his eyes. This was a small seizure, but after twenty-five years, it is the one I remember most. I remember that a side of me regretted the second search and almost wished I hadn't called "bingo" when I came across it. The man had a kind face, looked tired, and I knew that he was contemplating the sickness that would come over him on the jail cot.

Many of these old heroin addicts didn't end up on the Skids. The large shipments of heroin that make it through the ports and airports of Vancouver tell me that thousands of drug addicts fix every day and not all of them end up in the back alleys of East Hastings. The people I sat with in the Blackstone struggled and lived for their heroin fix and no one talked about quitting, even when they got hurt. From the first hit they took, they learned from each other, and no one else paid attention until the police and the courts came in. They built relationships over the years and lived a life ruled by addiction and all its hardships. Unless you are a policeman or an addiction clinic worker, or a parent, brother, or sister, you don't hear about most heroin users. They use the methadone program to fill the gaps and will sometimes sell to each other if they come across a supply. They don't get rich dealing, and they don't talk about getting off heroin.

A few months after I testified in Captain Kangaroo's trial, I decided to give him a call. There was at first silence at the other end, but he agreed to meet with me. A partner and I picked him up off the street in the south end of town on a quiet, rainy night. We found a dark place to park while chatting awkwardly.

"How have you been?" I asked.

"Good."

"It's good to see you."

We spoke of our time together in the Blackstone and I told

him that I was on the heroin unit. Sitting in our car, he knew that I wanted him to work with us. I told him that I understood what he dealt with every day and that I knew that, sometimes, things go wrong on the street. I offered no commitment and asked for none, but I knew that there was a sense of fairness in him, and that he may be inclined to do something about the violence and bad drugs hitting the street.

Kangaroo looked at me.

"What you said at the trial, I never saw a cop do that."

I had forgotten about it. In the eight months I was in the Blackstone, I saw Kangaroo deal only on a few occasions, just like most users, so when the prosecutor asked me if he played a major role on the street heroin scene, I answered "no." Kangaroo was let go with a small fine.

Kangaroo took a deep breath and swallowed hard, and then started to tell us what was happening on the street. In the times we met with him, Kangaroo never gave direct information about his suppliers, at least, not enough for an arrest. But combining his information with what we had helped us identify and take down aggressive dealers. It also gave us another finger on the pulse. We often chatted together about family. His wife was also a heroin user and their life was simple. She didn't know he talked to us. Kangaroo had a liver disease and passed away after I was transferred to another unit.

Speaking with old heroin informants opened my eyes to another face of addiction. We usually hear accounts of young heroin users who bottom-out before finding their way out of their addiction. But some of our informants were in their sixties and had worked with the police for decades, having gone through one team of handlers after another, making a few bucks here and there, and staying out of jail. True, hard addicts, they had learned to operate and survive the rip-offs, the bad or hot drugs, the violence of the street, and the police. They had gone in and out of jail, been sick plenty of times before settling into their habit, and found a way to make a go of it. Usually married to another addict, their friends were also users, and for the most part, they helped each other. There is a life to live even for heroin addicts.

Shortly after the operation, AIDS hit Vancouver in full force, decimating street workers and intravenous drug users. Crack cocaine and freebase, smokeable heroin offered a cheap way to get high, and more people died. In 1996, when I returned to Vancouver, cell phones turned the drug trade into a new game. You didn't need to have connections anymore. You called a number and a car would show up. Heroin was brought to small towns across the province, cheap and convenient. The same group would sell cocaine or heroin or both, all you had to say was "one-up" if you wanted coke, or "one-down" if you wanted heroin, and fifty dollars would get you high with either. More people died. Then, ecstasy became the drug of choice for partying teenagers, followed by crystal meth, each with its crisis, each with its number of deaths. Fentanyl is now the crisis, deadlier than its predecessors, adding to a multitude of opioids now on the street. Access is made easier every day by the connectivity of the internet, and new science will continue to bring more powerful drugs to anyone who wants them.

It is generally understood that with addiction, exposure, and easy access to the substance is directly related to the amount of use and damage. Accordingly, taking on organized crime to reduce supply has an impact whether we tackle drugs or money laundering, and this won't change. Rehabilitation and post-addiction harm reduction also play an important role in dealing with addicts who have bottomed out. But do we need to wait for the police or addiction centres to intervene before we do something about addiction? Addiction needs a new approach where drug awareness is replaced with self-awareness and support. We need to provide everyone with the tools to detect its early signs, and to provide mental health support regardless of age and type of addiction.

Good mental health care costs money, but still a lot less than what was spent on the war on drugs.

As today's technology rapidly brings new deadly products to the illicit drug market, we keep looking for solutions in the easiest places: in the eighties, it was the war on drugs and the "say no to drugs" programs. Today, harm reduction and safe injection sites make the headlines, while elemental mental health management is still merely an afterthought.

The Blackstone is really not different than any other place where people get together to get high. When I started working as a cop, my team usually got together for a beer after work, telling stories and winding down. A lot of it was good, but we often drank too much, and it caused damage to some of us, although no one spoke of it. Drugs and alcohol are present in all of our lives, whether we use them ourselves or not, with the good times mixing with the bad, but no one pays attention until things go off the rails and the police or rehab must intervene.

Coping with addiction is a personal journey taken by most people in their early years, whether it is gambling, caffeine, nicotine, sex, cocaine and heroin, alcohol, ecstasy, or prescription pills. It isn't about the substance, it is about addiction and its impact.

We learn on our own and it's not about the drug. It's about what goes on inside you when you know you like something too much. An early warning light comes on, strong and bright, and you still don't get it. As a cop, most of the misery I saw every day had to do with some substance or another, mainly alcohol. As an individual, I have seen people I care about hurt by it and regret not being there to help. As a society, there is nothing we can change until we learn to deal with addiction. Dealing with addiction is part of life and we need to be better at it.

Addiction is a part of us and we are all affected by it in one way or another. Yet, as a society, we treat it as if it didn't have anything to do with us. That it is a marginal problem. When I became a police officer in the late seventies, stopping an impaired driver was a casual, daily event. You only had to run a roadblock for a few minutes on any evening to find someone driving impaired. Everyone knew that it was wrong, but there was a general acceptance of it, as if it was okay as long as you didn't get caught or get into an accident. But then, spurred by the efforts of Mothers Against Drunk Driving (MADD), society changed and people were no longer afraid to bring up the issue and eventually make the police effort more effective. I cannot imagine anyone today telling the joke that "I drove because I was too drunk to walk," but back then, it made everyone laugh. Values and standards that society will support should be the driving force behind law enforcement, and not the other way around.

When I look back and see myself sitting at a table in the Blackstone with one of its heroin users, the time spent, over the years, discussing drug policies cease to resonate. Reducing supply helps, but we can't stop it all, especially if society accepts drug use; harm reduction is a lofty goal, but it only occurs after the harm is done. Addiction is a mental health issue that affects everyone differently and everybody should have, at the earliest stages, the knowledge to understand the effect it has on them, and to know where to go and what to do to deal with it. Drugs will come and go, some deadlier than others, but the pull of addiction will continue to creep into our lives as it has since the beginning of time. Law enforcement has a role to play but it needs to support, and be proportionate to, the will of the community. It needs to support a holistic approach that includes mental health, education, harm reduction, and serious community engagement. Viewed in the light of my own experience, I feel it important to look at addiction in a different way, perhaps in a place where we have not looked before.

ACKNOWLEDGEMENTS

My wife Sally was the first person to lay eyes on what was then still a rough draft of *Horseplay*. She is my strength and my compass and I am grateful for her unwavering support, from the first time she looked at the manuscript, to its final draft.

This book would also not be complete without an opportunity to express my gratitude to the many early readers who, on the basis of friendship alone, gave time and effort to help bring this story to its finished state. Special thanks to Peter and Frances O'Malley, Kevin and Tammy Lee, Jeannette Labelle, my daughter Valerie, and my son Stephen for their insightful feedback. Special thanks also to my editor Merrill Distad for his dedicated attention and wonderful instinct, and for making the process enjoyable, and to Claire Kelly and Matt Bowes at NeWest Press for their expert guidance and support through the publishing process.

Life in the RCMP is made of departures, and during my service I had the opportunity to work with and meet many great people before our careers took us in different directions. I am grateful to each one of you for your enduring friendship and for what I learned working at your side.

NORM BOUCHER left Montréal at the age of nineteen to begin a long and rewarding career as an RCMP officer mostly dedicated to drugs and organized crime. An active member of the RCMP undercover program for over ten years, his assignments included drug trafficking, money laundering, and homicide. He eventually represented the RCMP as a member of the Canadian delegation to several Regular Sessions of the Inter-American Drug Abuse Commission of the Organization of American States, held in Washington D.C. and Mexico City, where he helped develop a community policing program aimed at drug harm reduction. His varied career included postings on the national anti-terrorist Special Emergency Response Team, as Marine drug enforcement coordinator on Canada's West Coast, and as liaison officer in Madrid, Spain, and Santo Domingo, Dominican Republic.

In 1983, Staff-Sergeant Boucher spent eight months infiltrating the heart of Vancouver's heroin scene. This experience became the subject of his memoir *Horseplay: My Time Undercover on the Granville Strip*, which he wrote over a period of several years, while continuing to fulfill his RCMP responsibilities in Canada and abroad. In 2012, Norm Boucher retired from the RCMP as a Staff-Sergeant, dedicating his time to writing and his work as a consultant.

Norm Boucher studied literature at the University of Waterloo. He is the recipient of the Governor General's Medal of Bravery, the Carnegie Medal, and the Queen's Diamond Jubilee Medal. He is the proud father of four children and now lives in Manotick, Ontario with his wife Sally and their dog Cooper.